TENNESSEE
Off the Beaten Path

TENNESSEE
Off the Beaten Path

by
Tim O'Brien

A Voyager Book

The
Globe
Pequot
Press

Chester, Connecticut

Library of Congress Cataloging-in-Publication Data

O'Brien, Tim.
    Tennessee : off the beaten path / by Tim O'Brien. — 1st ed.
      p.   cm.
    "A Voyager book."
    ISBN 0-87106-484-7
    1. Tennessee—Description and travel—1981- —Guide-books.
I. Title.
F434.3.O27   1990
917.6084'53—dc20   89-78386
                                                             CIP

Cover illustration by M. A. Dube.
Text illustrations by Carole Drong.
Cover: Sam Houston Schoolhouse, Maryville, Tennessee.

Manufactured in the United States of America
First Edition/First Printing

To my parents, Jim and Ann, for instilling in me the wanderlust that has always given me the desire to travel the world's least-traveled byways.

Tennessee

Contents

The Lookout Mountain Incline Railway, Chattanooga

Introduction

The state of Tennessee is a fun state to explore. From the mountainous areas in the east to the delta plains of the Mississippi River in the west, the variety of natural wonders and attractions the state has to offer is awesome.

It would take volumes to detail all of Tennessee's highlights. In *Tennessee: Off the Beaten Path,* we've narrowed your choices down considerably by taking you off the interstates and onto the side roads, where the character of the state shines through.

The state is an easy one to get around in. Major highways and interstates are abundant, and even though you won't be spending much time on those behemoths, it's nice to know they're there if you have to make a quick escape back to civilization.

The Tennessee Scenic Parkway System covers 2,300 miles of primarily two-lane roads that connect the state's parks, major lakes, historical sites, recreational attractions, and this book's lesser-known attractions. The parkways are marked with a sign sporting a mockingbird, the state bird. They are mounted directly above the state highway designation numbers along the roads at key intersections.

If you follow the suggestions in this book, you'll find yourself driving up steep mountain roads, across rolling plains, over a few century-old bridges, and down many a gravel road. You'll also find yourself floating on a lake 300 feet below the earth's surface, playing miniature golf on the side of a mountain, and eating the world's sweetest-tasting, vilest-smelling vegetable.

As in any area with a great deal of tourist traffic, Tennessee has its share of tourist traps along the well-worn trails. Sometimes our trip down the less-traveled paths of the state will intersect with those trails in order to highlight an event, an attraction, or a person worth visiting. We have found that sometimes it's worth fighting a crowd to see something that we'll probably never get a chance to see again. You'll find many of those once-in-a-lifetime opportunities in Tennessee.

Music is a big attraction in the state. From the birthplace of the blues in Memphis to the birthplace of the Grand Ole Opry in Nashville to the songs of the Appalachian Mountain folks, music of all kinds has played an important part in the heritage of Tennessee. Our tour of the state will touch on much of that heritage and the people who have contributed to it. We'll visit the commercial monuments that honor Carl Perkins, Dolly Parton, Loretta Lynn, Conway Twitty, and many others.

Introduction

Southern hospitality is more than a myth in Tennessee, and our people may well be the state's friendliest attraction. There is one thing you'll never have to worry about as you travel through the state: You'll never truly be lost. Knock on any door or stop by any store, and chances are you'll get the directions you need, plus a whole lot more. Just when you think you've met the world's most colorful person, you'll meet one just a bit more fun. That's the way it is in Tennessee.

The state is full of crossroad communities with colorful and descriptive names. Usually, the community has little more to offer than a gas station–general store combination, but here's where you'll usually find the most intriguing characters of the area.

In the summer, these folks will be sitting on the porch of that store solving the world's problems. In the winter, you'll find them sitting around the pot-bellied stove. There are more than a hundred such communities around the state with colorful names, including Defeated, Fly, Yum Yum, Zu Zu, Lick Skillet, Skullbone, Nameless, Cornpone, Life, Only, Bucksnort, Sawdust, Frog Jump, Stupidville, Nosey Valley, and Difficult.

For tourism promotion purposes, state officials have divided the state into five major areas:

The First Frontier. More than 200 years ago, this part of the state was America's new frontier. Explorers, including Daniel Boone, blazed paths across the Appalachian Mountains, establishing some of the first settlements outside the original thirteen colonies.

Much of the area is heavily forested, with the extreme east and southern parts quite moutainous. Davy Crockett was born here, and the state of Franklin, which never quite made it to statehood, was formed here several years before Tennessee became a state.

The Mountainous East. As the name implies, this area is probably the most rugged of all Tennessee terrain. The 500,000-acre Great Smoky Mountain National Park and its foothill communities provide beauty incomparable to what you'll find elsewhere in the Southeast.

Throughout the area several museums have dedicated their collections and grounds to the preservation of mountain life, and many communities have preserved that life-style by their very existence.

Plateaus and Valleys. Forested and rugged, the Cumberland Plateau rises like a gigantic wall that spans the width of the state, forming the western boundary of the Tennessee Valley.

Although relatively flat, the area has many spectacular streams that have carved out deep gorges in the sandstone, making it one of the best areas in the state for white-water enthusiasts.

The Heartland. Also known as Middle Tennessee, the area is a region of gently rolling hills, sloping green meadows, and miles of river and lake frontage.

At the heart of the area lies Nashville, "Music City USA," the home of the Grand Ole Opry. Musical attractions are popular in this area, as are Tennessee Walking Horse farms, sour mash whiskey distilleries, and the homes of two U.S. presidents.

Western Plains. An area of fertile bottomlands and dense hardwood forests, the Western Plains is bordered on the east by the Tennessee River and on the west by the Mississippi.

A few of the state's most colorful folk heroes, frontiersman Davy Crockett, train engineer Casey Jones, and *Walking Tall* sheriff Buford Pusser, have strong roots here, as do *Roots* author Alex Haley and the King of Rock 'n' Roll, Elvis Presley.

The 520-mile-long state is divided into two telephone area codes, 901 and 615, and about half of it lies in the eastern time zone and half in the central zone.

While care has been taken to ensure accuracy in all listings in this book, visitors would be advised to call ahead before traveling any great distance. Life throughout Tennessee is slow paced and mellow, so if a day appears to be going a bit slow, it isn't uncommon for a proprietor to close early and go fishing. Phone numbers have been included in listings where appropriate.

Most of the attractions are open on a year-round basis, but some cut operations a bit during the winter months.

Before venturing forth, you may want to contact the state tourism bureau and load up on brochures and maps of the areas you plan on visiting. In the material you receive from the state, there will be a list of local tourism bureaus that will be able to provide even more specific information.

Write to Tennessee Tourist Development, P.O. Box 23170, Nashville, TN 37202, or call (615) 741–2158.

Note: Because of periodic price increases, admission prices to individual attractions have not been listed. The publisher recommends that readers call attractions before traveling to obtain current information.

Off the Beaten Path on the First Frontier

1. The Grand Guitar Museum
2. Ridgewood Restaurant
3. Iron Mountain Stoneware
4. Trade
5. The Kissing Bridge
6. Fudd's Old Country Store
7. Erwin
8. Old Town Hall
9. Parson's Table Restaurant
10. Davy Crockett Birthplace
    State Historical Area
11. Tusculum College
12. Tennessee Mountaineer
    Restaurant
13. Hale Springs Inn

The First Frontier

Sullivan County

Bristol is about as far north as one can go in the state and stay in Tennessee. In fact, about half the city is in Virginia. The state line runs down the middle of State Street in the heart of the downtown shopping district. But other than the small state markers embedded in the street between the double yellow lines, there's little evidence that the city has two mayors, two city councils, and two telephone area codes.

A big, old-fashioned neon sign forms an archway across State Street, near Randall Street, and proclaims "Bristol is a good place to live." Arrows point to the Tennessee and Virginia sides.

Although Nashville, about 300 miles to the west, gets credit for being the center of country music, it was here in Bristol that the Carter Family and Jimmie Rodgers recorded the first country-and-western music that was distributed nationwide. That recording took place on August 2, 1927, and put the area on the musical map. A monument honoring those musical pioneers stands at Edgemont Avenue and State Street. Farther down State Street, a large mural on the side of a building presents a visual memorial to that event.

Continue down State Street and take a right on Commonwealth Avenue. In about three blocks is an area known as the Commonwealth Antique Section. There, you'll find an antique mall and about a half-dozen other similiar shops.

In keeping with the musical heritage of the area, **The Grand Guitar Museum** is located at 535 New Kingsport Highway. Follow State Street out of downtown, and you'll see the museum in about 3½ miles, on the right. (The street turns into New Kingsport Highway once you leave downtown.) The building is built to resemble a guitar lying on its side and is said to be the only guitar-shaped building in America. Inside are several displays of rare stringed instruments and a gift shop. Open daily; admission free; (615) 968–1719.

In nearby Kingsport, early travelers through the area exchanged their Virginia currency for Tennessee money at a stagecoach stop known as the Exchange Place. Today, the small farmlike village and crafts center is open weekends during the warmer months. You'll usually find a group of ladies working on

2

The Grand Guitar Museum

a quilt outside under one of the large shade trees. The village is located just off Highway 11W, at 4812 Orebank Road. Admission free; (615) 288–6071.

Unlikely as it seems, a major U.S. boatyard was in operation along the Holston River here in Kingsport in 1802. William King's boatyard had a quality reputation that stretched as far as New Orleans. On the hill across the stagecoach road from the yards was the always-busy Netherland Inn, an inn and tavern where the likes of the state's three presidents, Andrew Jackson, Andrew Johnson, and James K. Polk, whiled away hours with their friends. The inn has been restored and is open to the public as a museum. Several other buildings on the property, including a shop and wagon shelter, have also been restored. A log cabin that was moved here from Virginia and once served as Daniel Boone's home from 1773 to 1775 is now a children's museum; it is a must if there are any small travelers with you. The boatyards are now a city park that stretches for miles down the river. Admission charged to the museum; (615) 247–3211.

The city fathers of Blountville say that there are more original log houses along their city's main street than in any other town in the state. Whether that's true or not, there are a great many vintage buildings to see here. One of those, The Deery Inn, played an important part in the frontier era of this part of the state. Built during the late 1700s, the building is actually three buildings: a two-story hewn-log house, a three-story cut-stone house, and a two-story frame structure, all built adjacent to one another and joined together. It's now a private residence, but according to the local librarian, the lady who lives there "has been known to allow interested people to walk through the structure."

Across the street is the Cannonball House Antiques and Gifts shop. This old structure got its name for a big cannonball hole that still exists in the building.

A walking-tour map of Blountville is available, and most of the buildings are decorated and open to the public around Christmas.

Continue on Highway 37 out of Blountville and head south to Bluff City. Just as you cross the Boone Lake bridge coming into town, look to your left and you'll see this community's answer to what to do with old railroad abutments. The trestle has been removed and a mural painted on the stone wall. The colorful painting depicts a train coming out of a tunnel. It's a nice touch.

For the best barbecue meal in eastern Tennessee, continue through Bluff City and head out Highway 19E. There you'll find the **Ridgewood Restaurant.** Grace Proffitt and her restaurant are legendary in these parts. She has been dishing up barbecued pork and beef since 1948, and most barbecue experts from coast to coast agree that hers is some of the best in the country.

Much of the cooking is done out front where patrons can watch. Although many other items take up space on the menu, it's the barbecue that brings people through the doors. She makes about sixteen gallons of her special sweet-and-sour sauce a day. "It's a secret recipe, and I keep it in my head," she claims. Her son Terry, who works the eatery with her, is the only other person who knows the exact blends.

Coleslaw is put on all barbecue sandwiches, and various other hot sauces accompany hers to the table. Great northern white beans are prepared in her sauce and served along with hand-cut french fries on the popular platters. No reservations are taken, and the weekends tend to get crowded. Open every day but Monday; (615) 538–7543.

Perhaps one of the most historically significant extant structures in the state is Rocky Mount, a two-story log cabin in Piney Flats. Built in 1770, Rocky Mount is the oldest original territorial capital in the United States and one of the oldest buildings in the state.

It was the capital of "The Territory of the United States south of the river Ohio" from 1790 until a new capitol was built in Knoxville. With two stories and nine rooms, pine paneling, and real glass windows, the structure was a mansion by frontier standards, and it quickly became a gathering place for people across the entire frontier.

Today, the house is open to the public daily, as is the adjoining Overmountain Museum, which shows the early life of the area. On Route 11E; (615) 538–7396.

Johnson County

This county is surrounded by the hills of the Appalachian Mountains, and the businesses and attractions reflect that way of life quite nicely. Throughout the county you'll see small handwritten signs hanging from mailboxes advertising handmade quilts or birdhouses for sale. Farther down any road, you'll pass through a crossroads community with a small general store stocked with local Appalachian crafts.

In Mountain City, about the only thing you won't find are crowds. Granny's Hope Chest, at 308 South Church Street, specializes in vintage clothing, linen, and jewelry. You might not always find Granny there, but if she has to step out during the day, she'll leave her door unlocked for you.

Hidden Treasures, The Hitching Post, and the Mill Outlet are other quaint shopping establishments all within a two-block area in the downtown section.

North of Mountain City, on Highway 91, is Laurel Bloomery, a small community of about seventy people. There, **Iron Mountain Stoneware** makes its world-famous line, which can be found in posh department stores across the country, including Tiffany's in New York City. More than 600 stores sell the products created here at the foot of Iron Mountain.

Iron Mountain is one of the few firms in the country that still produces high-fired stoneware dinnerware. Most of the work is done by hand, but the owners say that just enough mechanization is used to keep the process efficient. "We do everything here but mine the clay," said Joe Lamb, the plant's engineer. The pottery operates an on-site retail store that carries a full line of the nineteen separate patterns they create. Special discount sales are held each year at Mother's Day and Thanksgiving.

The tours are informal and are often given by the firm's founder, president, and resident artist, Nancy Lamb; (615) 727–8888.

South of Mountain City on Highway 421 is **Trade,** the oldest unincorporated community in the state. It's the spot where the first English-speaking white man set foot on Tennessee soil in 1673. Situated on an old buffalo trail, the community flourished as a resting place for those traveling the three major paths through the wilderness that crossed at this point.

By the 1790s, the area had a country store, a post office, a blacksmith shop, and a handful of cabins, and today it's about as low-key as it was then—no big signs and no souvenir shops. "Trade Days" is held each June, when the entire county comes out to celebrate the heritage of the area.

A few miles outside of Trade, on Route 67, Jack Belk has his Casa Que Pasa antique shop, and it's exactly what you'd expect out here in the mountains. He specializes in vintage quilts, stained-glass windows, antique furniture, primitives, and art deco. Next door is Frank's Antiques, chock-full of tools, farm-related antiques, kerosene lanterns, and buggy wheels.

Carter County

One of the state's remaining original covered bridges crosses the Doe River in downtown Elizabethton and is the focal point for the city's riverside park. Built in 1882, **The Kissing Bridge** (as the locals call it) is the oldest such structure in the state.

For many years, a tall Frazier fir tree on Elk Street near downtown Elizabethton was considered the tallest such tree in the world. Then the gloomy day came when officials found it was only the second tallest. But since the tallest is never decorated at Christmas, they now decorate the fir in Elizabethton, making it the tallest *decorated* Frazier fir tree in the world.

Flying missionaries to and from remote parts of the world is quite difficult and requires pilots trained in a "seat of your pants" style of piloting. In Elizabethton, Moody Missionary Aviation trains pilots to do just that. A division of Chicago's Moody Bible Institute, the aviation school provides three years of technical training for a student who has already completed two years of missionary studies.

Once students graduate, they are "free agents" who can work

for any missionary organization. "Our pilots are capable of flying in the worst of conditions with no instruments and, most often, no formal landing strip," said flight instructor Bruce Hendrich. "And since they are also trained missionaries, they understand the importance of their jobs."

The school also functions as a "regular" flight school and operates a charter service. In addition, it is under contract with the city of Elizbethton to run the city airport. The entire operation is open for public tours, and plane rides of the mountainous areas are available from here; (615) 543–3534.

About 20 miles southeast of Elizabethton on Highway 143 is Roan Mountain State Park. The park itself lies at the foot of Roan Mountain, one of the highest peaks (6,313 feet) in the Eastern United States, but that's not what makes this park so special. On the side of that mountain is one of the largest rhododendron gardens in the country. More than 600 acres of color bloom each aone of tJune, making the area a striking display of pinks and purples. The park is he best places in the area to view fall foliage. A campground and cabins offer overnighters grand vistas of the mountains.

Walking and hiking trails line the mountain with numerous "scenic overlooks." The Dave Miller Homestead, a preserved farm, is located in the park in a hollow atop Strawberry Mountain. The Miller family first settled in the area around 1870 and for generations lived in virtual seclusion. Today, the farm is preserved intact and serves as a model of early Appalachian life. Frank Miller, grandson of Dave, is the caretaker and is eager to share his knowledge and humor with visitors. Admission free; (615) 772–3303.

It's hard to miss **Fudd's Old Country Store,** 3 miles west of Elizabethton on Highway 321. A long, old building and various outbuildings, including the house that President Andrew Johnson died in on July 3, 1875, are lined up along the right side of the road. Phil Campbell, who runs the store with his mother, Arlene, says he specializes in everything, but he has a hard time trying to sell anything new. "We have antiques, collectibles, and some craft items," he says.

In addition to the retail business, Phil has created a museum in honor of his father, Fudd Campbell, which contains more than 15,000 items. "Dad collected everything that was peculiar," Phil admits. In the museum are artifacts from an early Woodland Indian burial pit, found on the property when Fudd started building the structures; pieces from the county's first bank; old coffins; a gristmill; and a moonshine still. Other items range from baby dolls to oxen shoes to strawberry capper scissors. Admission free.

The Johnson home isn't open to tour, but you can look through the open doors and see the period furnishings. Next to that house is a 200-year-old log-cabin church with log pews and a pump organ that works. This eclectic attraction is open six days a week, closed Sundays. "We're not fancy here, but you'll find a whole lot of things those fancy museums haven't even heard of," says Phil. (615) 543–8618.

Farther down Highway 321 toward Johnson City is the Sinking Creek Baptist Church. The log structure, built in 1803, is the oldest Baptist church in the state and is open to the public on weekdays during the warmer months. It's located next to the new church; (615) 928–3222.

Unicoi County

The county seat community of **Erwin** probably holds the distinction of being the only town ever to put an elephant on trial for murder, find it guilty, and carry out the death penalty.

"Big Mary," a circus elephant who trampled her owner to death, was hanged from a railroad derrick before 5,000 spectators in 1916. Newspaper clippings and photos of that event are but a few of the interesting items in the Unicoi County Heritage Museum, housed in a turn-of-the-century home on the grounds of the National Fish Hatchery on Highway 23.

The hatchery was established in 1894, and the ten-room superintendent's residence was constructed in 1903. By the early 1980s, the house wasn't being used by the superintendent, so the federal government signed an agreement allowing the county to use it as a museum. In addition to the story of Big Mary, various displays highlight local pottery production, the history of local railroading, and on the second floor is a replica of the city's turn-of-the-century Main Street.

In "Grandmother's Attic" is a display of quilts, antique dolls, and children's toys, all displayed as they might be in your own grandma's attic.

Outside, the fish hatchery is still in operation and produces about 18 million rainbow trout eggs each year. Tours are available at the hatchery as well as at the museum. Admission free; (615) 743–4712 for the hatchery, (615) 743–9449 for the museum.

Bring your lunch; the entire area is a beautiful parklike setting, complete with a picnic pavilion and rest rooms.

Washington County

The sixteen counties that now make up the eastern tip of Tennessee were at one time united together in an effort to become a state by themselves. The framework for the state of Franklin was set when about 30,000 white settlers crossed the Appalachian Mountains and founded several settlements in this area, which was a part of North Carolina at the time.

Leaders met in Jonesborough and created a bill of rights for their new state and requested the lawmakers of North Carolina to allow the new state. They refused, but Franklin, under the leadership of John Sevier, continued the battle for several years, until 1788. Several skirmishes between Franklin and North Carolina militia took place in the area.

Although never recognized as an official state, Franklin operated like a sovereign government with an assembly, administered justice, and negotiated treaties with the Indians.

Eight years after the fight for the quasi-state ended, Sevier became the first governor of the state of Tennessee, which incorporated the former boundaries of Franklin. Jonesborough, chartered in 1779, seventeen years before there was a Tennessee, holds the distinction of being the oldest incorporated area in the state. And thanks to an ambitious restoration effort, much of the city appears as it did more than a century ago.

There are more than twenty-seven points of interest on the walking-tour map of the historic downtown area, including the historic Chester Inn, where a young Andrew Jackson stayed while working on his law degree in 1788.

Many of the old buildings along the main streets now house a wide array of specialty shops. One particular structure, the **Old Town Hall,** at 144 East Main Street, was restored in 1982 and now houses about fifty crafts-oriented shops, plus a small deli restaurant. Down the street is "Mauk's (more than a) Pharmacy." Considered the state's oldest continuously operating drug store, the business has been in the same family since 1891.

Over behind the courthouse, at 102 Woodrow Avenue, the **Parson's Table Restaurant** is located in the circa-1870 First Christian Church building and parsonage. Owned by Debra and "Chef"

Jeff Myron, the Victorian dining hall offers classical music, linen tablecloths and napkins, and about twenty entrees for dinner every night except Monday. A Sunday buffet is served and there is a daily luncheon special. This is truly an oasis of elegant dining among the barbecue restaurants of eastern Tennessee. Complete dinners range from $10 to $20. No alcohol is sold, but bring your own wine and they'll keep it chilled for you. Reservations suggested for dinner; (615) 753–8003.

The Old Masonic Hall at 129 East Main Street is now the home of the Old Sweet Shop and the best ice cream concoctions in the area. The building once housed the only lodge in America with both its founding documents: the dispensation and the charter signed by President Andrew Jackson. Open daily; (615) 753–8851.

Tobie Bledsoe owns several historic buildings in the downtown area and has turned three of them into the best bed-and-breakfast facilities in town. All are within walking distance of the rest of the historic district. (615) 753–9223.

The Jonesborough–Washington County History Museum, at 117 Boone Street, also serves as a visitors center and is a good place to start your visit to this historic area. Brochures, maps, and a short film will get you started in the right direction. Make sure you pick up a free copy of "An Introduction to Building Watching," a guide on how to get the most out of viewing historic structures. It really is helpful, even if you think you already know architecture. Open daily; (615) 753–5961.

Greene County

Contrary to the myth started by Walt Disney, Davy Crockett was not born on a mountaintop in Tennessee; he was born along the banks of Nolichuckey River, near the mouth of Limestone Creek. Today that birth spot, just outside of the small community of Limestone, is marked by the **Davy Crockett Birthplace State Historical Area.**

Born in 1786, David (he never signed his name Davy) went on to become the "King of the Wild Frontier." His name and legend can rightfully be claimed by many areas in the state. He was born here in the east, he ran a gristmill in the center of the state, and he was elected to Congress from western Tennessee.

But here is where it all began. A reproduction of his birthplace cabin has been constructed, with the cornerstone of his original

Davy Crockett's Birthplace, Limestone

cabin on display. Probably the most unusual aspect of this park is the monument erected in the late 1960s by a local civic organization. In honor of Crockett's stature as a national hero, each of the fifty states is represented in the wall of the monument. Stones native to each state are incorporated in the wall and engraved with the respective state's name.

The park, located about 3¹/₂ miles from Highway 321, has a campground, swimming pool, picnic facilities, and a visitors center. Open year-round; cabin open daily during the warmer months; (615) 257–2061.

Within walking distance of the park is the Snapp Inn Bed and Breakfast. Owned by Dan and Ruth Dorgan, the inn is a restored 1815 Federal brick home, chock-full of antiques. Rates are $40 single, $50 double, and include a full breakfast. Nonsmoking patrons only; (615) 257–3986.

Fifteen minutes down Highway 321 is the county seat city of Greeneville, which happens to be the only Greeneville in the United States that uses that middle *e* in its name.

It was to this city that an eighteen-year-old boy moved in 1826 to establish a tailor business for himself. Several years later, that boy, Andrew Johnson, became the country's seventeenth president. Today, Johnson's Greeneville years are highlighted at the Andrew Johnson National Historic Site, in the downtown section. His small tailor shop has been preserved and is inside the site's visitors center. Across the street is the brick home in which he lived, and the cemetery where he and his family are buried is a few miles away. All three attractions are open every day except Christmas Day. The visitors center is located at the corner of College and Depot streets; (615) 638–3551.

Across College Street from the Johnson site is the Ye Olde Tourist Trappe crafts cooperative. Managed by Nancy McNeese, the shop features works from more than sixty local craftspeople and includes everything from quilts to wooden toys to wreaths to cookbooks of local delicacies. Open daily; (615) 639–1567.

A walking-tour map of Greeneville is available that highlights thirty-six historic areas or structures of the community, including St. James Episcopal Church, circa 1850. Its interior is exceptional, with walnut woodwork and pews, a slave gallery, and the oldest working organ in the state. (615) 638–4111.

Greeneville's **Tusculum College,** founded in 1794, is the oldest college south of the Ohio River and west of the Allegheny Mountains. It was the twenty-eighth college founded in America, is the oldest college in the state, and is the oldest coed college associated with the Presbyterian Church.

Eight buildings on the campus were constructed between 1841 and 1928 and comprise the college's historic district. A walking tour of the campus is included in the city's walking-tour brochure.

The college's Andrew Johnson Library and Museum is the state's largest presidential library and houses a great many of the president's books, papers, and manuscripts, as well as those of his family. In addition, the library houses almost 200 original Civil War–era newspapers from throughout the country. (615) 638–1111.

Five miles southeast of town on Highway 70 the University of Tennessee has an experimental farm that specializes in research on burly tobacco. The farm, according to Phil Hunter, its superintendent, concentrates on developing disease-resistant varieties and on labor-saving production practices. The fall is the best time to visit the farm. That's when the cutting, handling, and drying procedures are undertaken, but Hunter assures us that if you're not familiar with tobacco production, a trip to the farm anytime would be quite fascinating. Tobacco is the leading cash crop of Tennessee, which is the third largest tobacco producer in the country. (615) 638–6532.

Hawkins County

The **Tennessee Mountaineer Restaurant,** on Highway 11W in Church Hill, specializes in Hillbilly Fried Chicken. "It's not the way we fix them that's so special," said owner Clarence Painter. "It's the chickens themselves. They have one leg shorter than the other so they can walk on the side of the mountains around here."

Whether you believe that or not, you can believe that only good food is served up in this family restaurant. One indication that the food and environment are good is that this eatery is the meeting spot for five civic organizations and two hunting groups.

Make sure you leave room for dessert. Clarence's kitchen turns out peach cobbler, hot fudge cake, and chocolate pie. As a side dish, ask for the fried apples; they are prepared in a great-tasting blend of maple syrup and brown sugar. Open daily at 6:00 A.M.; (615) 357–5511. Before you leave, pick up a free copy of the mountain-talk primer that Clarence keeps near the cash register. Read and memorize it, and you'll be able to communicate with the mountain folk during the rest of your journey across Tennessee.

In downtown Rogersville, the **Hale Springs Inn** is considered to be the oldest continuously operating inn in the state. Built in 1824, the inn has been totally restored and today offers a dining room and eight guest rooms, all with fireplaces. Much of the original 1824 structure is evident, including the staircases and the wooden floors throughout. Each room is furnished with antique furniture. All three Tennessee presidents, Johnson, Jackson, and Polk, stayed here, and all have guest rooms named after them. Room rates range from $35 to $60, which includes breakfast. (615) 272–5171.

Down the street from the inn is the 1890 railroad depot. Located on Depot Street, at the railroad, the structure was renovated in 1989 and now holds the county history museum, the chamber of commerce, and the visitors center.

Most of the old structures in downtown Rogersville have been restored, and the entire district is on the National Register of Historic Places. A walking tour of the historic district includes the Hawkins County Courthouse. Built in 1836, the building is the oldest original courthouse still in use in the state.

Most of the Main Street retail businesses now sell antiques or crafts but there are still a few old-time offices and clothing stores along the way.

13

Hancock County

Scott Collins works at the courthouse in Sneedville, and he's considered to be a member of the nation's smallest minority. He's a Melungeon, and there are not too many true Melungeons left.

No one, not even Collins, knows where the Melungeon race came from, how they got here, or how far their ancestors go back. But during their heyday the center of their life was in this county, high atop Newman's Ridge. There are several theories on where the group came from, but the most widely accepted is that they are all descendants from a group of Portuguese sailors who sought freedom and deserted their ship in North Carolina.

Characteristically, Melungeons had smooth olive-colored skin, straight black hair, dark eyes, and high cheek bones. The women were shorter than average, and the men were tall and straight.

Because of mixed marriages during the 200 years or so the Melungeons called this area home, there are no "true" members of the race. "There are no distinctive traits evident in us today that make us look any different than anyone else," Collins said.

Up on Newman's Ridge today, you'll find a few old, grown-over buildings, and a cemetery. There are no good roads to get there, and most of the year it takes a four-wheel-drive vehicle to do so.

Collins is kind of the unofficial historian of the race as well as the area, and his office wall is covered with photos dating back to before 1900. Researching his race is almost impossible, since the county courthouse burned down twice during the years, destroying all records. Call Collins at the courthouse when you're in town, and he'll be glad to invite you over to see the photos and to talk about the Melungeons. (615) 733–4254.

You have to be going to Sneedville to get there. No major highways lead there, and there are only three state highways in the entire county. In a way, the area is a part of the state that time has forgot. There aren't too many pre-1900 structures in the county, and most of Sneedville proper reminds you of the 1950s.

The county received its first national food franchise in mid-1989, a Hardees restaurant. All other businesses are local, family-owned establishments. Total county population is about 7,000.

Off the Beaten Path in the Mountainous East

1. World's Largest Stalagmite
2. Lincoln Memorial University
3. The Murrell Flyer
4. Moonshine Capital of the World
5. Davy Crockett's Marriage License
6. LeConte Lodge
7. Hillbilly Golf Course
8. Dollywood
9. Giant Cuckoo Clock
10. Sunsphere
11. Little River Railroad and Lumber Company
12. The Lost Sea
13. Crosseyed Cricket
14. World's Smallest Library
15. Rugby's Utopian Community
16. "Secret City"
17. American Museum of Science and Energy
18. Museum of Appalachia
19. Lenoir Family Museum
20. Big South Fork River and Recreation Area

The Mountainous East

Claiborne County

The quaint little village of Cumberland Gap rests just a few miles from one of the most historic natural passageways of all times. Much of the westward movement of early America came through this V-shaped indentation in the Appalachian Mountain chain, a wall of rock that stretches from Maine to Georgia.

It was 1775 when Daniel Boone and his thirty axmen hacked out the Wilderness Road through the gap to open up the "western frontier" and the fertile farm lands on the other side. It was the first road platted by a white man in the state. That byway became a major thoroughfare and is now a four-lane highway.

At the top of the gap, a marker in the Cumberland Gap National Historic Park shows where the states of Kentucky, Virginia, and Tennessee meet. It is said that from the top, those three states, plus Georgia and North Carolina, can be seen on a clear day. A visitors center and museum are part of the park. (606) 248–2817.

Directly below that point, deep beneath the mountain, the **World's Largest Stalagmite** can be found in Cudjo's Caverns. It's 65 feet high, 35 feet in circumference, and still growing. Officials say the formation, which they call the "Pillar of Hercules," is approximately eighty-five million years old. Admission charged; (703) 861–2203.

The village of Cumberland Gap was founded by English settlers and today shows a strong English influence in its architecture. The downtown section has been virtually untouched by modernization for fifty years. The opening scene of a movie was filmed here in 1988, and according to one of the downtown businessmen, only one sign had to be removed to make the town look like a small town in the 1930s.

A few miles south on Highway 25E is Harrogate, the home of **Lincoln Memorial University.** Founded in 1896 as a living memorial to President Lincoln, the school's charter mandated the establishment of a museum to house memorabilia of the Lincoln era. Today, the Lincoln Library and Museum on the campus houses the third largest collection of Lincolniana and Civil War items in the world.

One of the most historic items in the museum is the ebony cane the president was carrying on the night he was assassinated. The school itself is beautiful and is a nice tribute to mountain life in east Tennessee. Take time to walk through the campus. Admission charged to museum; (615) 869–3611.

Farther south on Highway 25E near Tazewell is the Springdale Old Log Church. Built in 1795, a year before Tennessee became a state, the church is still the site of Baptist services one Sunday a month. (615) 626–4149.

Grainger County

When Andrew Johnson came to Tennessee to establish a tailor shop, he spent a few months in Rutledge before relocating to nearby Greeneville. A reproduction of Johnson's first shop has been built and is located in front of the Grainger County Courthouse, on the original site.

A few blocks away is the circa-1848 Grainger County Jail, the oldest standing brick jailhouse in Tennessee. Restored by the county's historical society, the facility now houses the society and serves as a public meeting house for the area's clubs and organizations. Inside, the original metal stairs and wall partitions are intact. Although not open on a regular basis, Virginia Leedy will be glad to show you around and tell you about the hanging just outside the front door. (615) 767–2376.

Near Washburn, Ann Stover Hurst has a cottage industry called the Shenanndoah Farm. There, she makes brooms and mops entirely by hand in the old Appalachian style, with natural vine and root handles. No machinery is used at all, making each creation unique. She also grows and packages herbs and produces pencil sketches of early mountain life. (615) 497–2608.

Hamblen County

In the 1790s, Davy Crockett's dad opened a small, six-room tavern near present-day Morristown. That's where little Davy spent his early years. In the 1950s a reproduction of that tavern was built on the original site, and today the David Crockett Tavern and Museum serves as a frontier museum honoring the Crockett family and other early Tennessee pioneers. The tavern is full of period utensils and furnishings. It's located at 2002 East Morningside Drive. (615) 581–8585.

The first patented flying machine in America was developed by

17

Melville Murrell, a Morristown preacher. Patented in 1877, a good while before the Wright Brothers, the **Murrell Flyer** flew several hundred yards under bicycle-type power. Parts of the original flyer, including its wings and some of the frame, are on display at the city's Rose Center. A video presentation features interviews with some of Murrell's descendants and several photos of the plane itself.

Built in 1892 and saved from destruction in 1975 by a community action group, the Rose Center was the area's first school. It now serves as a community cultural center and includes a history museum, art gallery, exhibit space, and gift shop. (615) 581–4330.

Each October, the Mountain Makin's Festival is held on the grounds of the Rose Center and features one of east Tennessee's finest juried crafts shows. Two music stages feature various forms of local mountain music and other activities. (615) 586–6382.

Cocke County

Cosby was settled in 1783 by a corn farmer searching for a quiet, peaceful life. Corn remained the main crop for many years, and it didn't take long before the discovery was made that it was easier to transport it in the liquid form known as moonshine. For many years, the area was known as the **"Moonshine Capital of the World."**

Today, the unincorporated downtown of Cosby consists of a post office, bar, bank, a small grocery store, and a gas station. In the hollow bordering the Great Smoky Mountain National Park, the area is still peaceful and quiet. The Schilling family's Folk Life Center, about a mile from downtown on Highway 32, is advertised as the "kind of shop you hope to find when you visit the Smokies." The family makes and plays dulcimers, but the store also sells crafts and products from more than 100 local craftspeople. (615) 487–5543.

Apples are now considered one of the area's biggest cash crops, and there are five or six major orchards that sell directly from their farms. Also, many smaller orchards have been planted and produce excellent crops. Look for "Apples For Sale" signs along the roads. One of the area's oldest orchards is owned and operated by the third generation of Baxters, out Highway 73 from Cosby; they sell cider and a home blend of honey that can't be beat.

The *ramp* is an onionlike vegetable native to the foothills of the southern Appalachian Mountains. The odd-looking plant has been described as the "vilest-smelling, sweetest-tasting vegetable in the world." Early settlers attributed special medicinal qualities to the ramp.

Raw, parboiled, fried, or scrambled in eggs, it was regarded as a necessary spring tonic to ward off the sluggishness of winter. In the 1950s Cosby introduced the ramp to the rest of the world when it established its first annual spring festival in the plant's honor. Each spring, thousands come here to enjoy activities and truckloads of ramps.

Frederich and Maria Marx, owners of Fort Marx, sold their restaurant and moved out into the country to retire. But the fans of their old establishment followed them, and it wasn't long before the Marxes were dishing up some of their fine German foods and serving "friends" out of their double-wide mobile home.

The crowds grew, and Frederich kept building onto the trailer. Today, Fort Marx serves the best German food in this part of the state. "We are known around the world," Frederich is quick to point out. "We've had people in here from every major country in the world, and I can prove it." He dusts off a series of guest books and starts pointing out the various visitors, along with stories on each one.

The menu, hand printed and stapled onto the wall, has an additional sign hanging from the bottom: "Maria can cook anything that walks, crawls, flies, or swims. But no oysters or clams, please. If it ain't on the menu, ask fer it."

The small funky restaurant can seat forty-five patrons. "And that has actually happened a time or two," Frederich adds. They've been here for twelve years, halfway up a hill above the Little Pigeon River. No road signs, only their name on the mailbox, a few miles off Wilton Springs Road, near Exit 440 off Interstate 40. (615) 487–2112.

In the county seat city of Newport, the Cocke County Museum is located upstairs in the Community Center building. Downstairs are the chamber of commerce and tourist information offices. This is a good place to start a tour of the county.

Jefferson County

One of the world's twenty-eight *ligors* lives on the Sklar Farm, 6 miles west of Newport on Highway 25/70, right on the county line. Benu, the half tiger, half lion is owned by Mary Ann Sklar and her daughter Rosemary. They run the exotic animal farm, which not only provides animals for movies and exhibitions but also has a petting zoo open to the public. Among the other animals at the farm are Australian wallabies, emus, llamas, parrots, and lions. Admission charged; (615) 397–3276.

Dandridge, the second oldest city in the state, is also the only city in the United States named for Martha Dandridge Washington, wife of our first president. The Jefferson County Museum, located on the first level of the circa-1845 county courthouse, has a good collection of regional history, including **Davy Crockett's Marriage License.** Admission free; open during courthouse hours; (615) 397–3800.

Information on the walking tour of downtown Dandridge, which features more than thirty structures on the National Historic Register, is available from the courthouse as well as from many stores throughout the area.

The Glenmore Mansion is considered by many architects as an almost perfect example of Victorian architecture. Built in 1869, the twenty-seven–room, five-story mansion is fully furnished with antiques of the period. In eastern Tennessee, where most historical preservation efforts are saved for pre-1850 architecture, it's good to see the preservation of the Victorian era. Located on Gibson Highway in Jefferson City; open Saturday and Sunday afternoons; (615) 397–9642.

In the southwestern part of the county on Highway 411, Chestnut Hill was begun as a company town. A. J. Bush was a schoolteacher and a general-store owner when he created a business to help provide the local men a chance for employment. A. J. Bush & Co. was founded in 1907 as a tomato processing plant. Today, there are eight plants processing canned vegetables that serve about 75 percent of the country.

Remnants of early Chestnut Hill are still evident. On the edge of town, there are still several early company houses being lived in. The general store at the gates of the plant is still there and sells "just about everything." During the 1920s and 1930s, the Bush family paid its employees partially in cash and partially in scrip, redeemable for merchandise and food at the company's general store.

J. C. Thornton, who started with the company during the war when he was fourteen, is considered the unofficial historian of the company and the town and is willing to share his stories with anyone who is interested. Public tours of the plant are not allowed because of insurance regulations, but J. C. has plenty of photos. Call first; (615) 623–2361.

Sevier County

As the most visited national park in the country with ten million visitors a year, the Great Smoky Mountains National Forest is hardly off the beaten path. But the facility is so large at 500,000 acres and has so many nooks and crannies that it isn't difficult to get away from the madding crowds.

There are established camping areas throughout the park, but camping is also permitted in the undeveloped regions as well. Special backcountry permits are needed for that.

The Sugarland's Visitors Center is located 2 miles inside the park from Gatlinburg and has maps and other information about the entire park, as well as exhibits on what one will most likely see during a visit.

Featuring more species of plants than any other area on our continent, this official International Biosphere Reserve is a true gem in Tennessee travel opportunities.

Within the boundaries, there are sixteen peaks towering above 6,000 feet, including Clingman's Dome, which, at 6,643 feet, is the highest point in Tennessee.

One of the park's most unusual attractions is **LeConte Lodge,** a great place to stay while in the mountains if you enjoy walking. In fact, that's the only way you can get there, and it's not the easiest walk you'll ever make. The lodge rests on top of the third highest peak in the park, making it the highest guest lodge in the Eastern United States. The shortest (and steepest) hike to the lodge is 5 1/2 miles long.

Another rustic but more accessible lodge is the Wonderland Hotel, which features a front porch lined with old-fashioned rockers and a magnificent view. A sign at the door proudly reads: "We have no radio, no TV and no telephone in every room."

Cades Cove was a thriving mountain community in the 1850s, with about 685 residents and 15,000 acres of usable farmland under cultivation. Today the area is as it was then, with original buildings in original locations, so the visitor can get a true sense of the spaciousness of early mountain life. An 11-mile self-guided

**Cades Cove Grist Mill
Great Smoky Mountain National Park**

auto loop tour gives the best idea of the culture of the region. Most homes, churches, and stores are open to the public and are accessible by dirt paths.

It's easy to get to the scenic panoramas in the park; there are plenty of designated pull-offs and observation areas. The Foothill Parkway provides some of the best sight-seeing from your auto, and possibly the best view in the park comes after a short walk through the wilderness to the observation tower at Clingman's Dome.

The tourist destination city of Gatlinburg is located near the main entrance to the park and is considered its main gateway. Souvenir and craft shops and various attractions line the main streets, while honeymoon houses and motels line the back streets.

Among the attractions, there are a few gems: If you happen to be one of the growing corps of people who love the macabre, a trip to the Seven Gables Haunted House is a must. It's on the

Parkway (main strip), a block from Ripley's Believe It or Not, up from the Guinness World Records Exhibition Center, and down from the Mysterious Mansion.

Since parking is at such a premium in Gatlinburg, perhaps the best deal in town is the 25-cent ride on its rapid transit system, the trolley. During peak season, the entire city can become one large parking lot, so find a place to park on the edge of town or at your hotel and rely on the trolley.

The **Hillbilly Golf Course** may well be one of the most unusual miniature golf courses in the world. To get to the first hole, you must ride an incline up to a point 300 feet above the city. Two 18-hole courses, with all sorts of mountaineer hazards, including a genuine outhouse, are carved out of the mountainside. (615) 436–7470.

America's first Motion Master Moving Theater opened for business in late 1989 and is the most unusual family attraction the city has to offer. A wide screen, individual computer-controlled seat movement, and "surround sound" all help create a you-are-there sensation. Theatergoers experience the jolts, bumps, and hairpin turns of adventures such as monster roller coasters and dune buggy races. (615) 436–9763.

Head north on Route 441 out of Gatlinburg, go through a part of the national forest, and 5 miles later, you'll be in Pigeon Forge. Similar to Gatlinburg in its attractions, this city's main draw is country singer Dolly Parton's theme park, **Dollywood.** Country music prevails in the park, as do country crafts and good country cooking. It's easy to find: turn east at the largest billboard in town, at the corner of Dollywood Lane. The park's welcome center, with a steam engine out front, is located under the sign.

The Dixie Stampede has an interesting concept for a southern dinner theater. While eating a southern feast, patrons watch a live show in the central dirt-covered arena. The Western show features thirty horses, Conestoga wagons, pig racing, bull riding, steer wrestling, and a bunch more good-old-boy activities. For added flavor, the Northerners sit on one side, the Southerners on the other. Reservations are sometimes necessary; (615) 453–4400.

Across the Parkway from the Factory Merchants Mall, you can pan for your own treasures at The Mine. Rubies, sapphires, and other precious stones are mixed with the dirt, and it's finders keepers. A gem shop is next door for those who want their finds mounted in earrings or rings. (615) 453–7712.

At the Bavarian Haus in Bell Tower Square, located next to the Pigeon Forge Welcome Center, a **Giant Cuckoo Clock,** billed as

23

the world's largest, goes into action every fifteen minutes. Five-foot-tall wooden musicians play while a 3-foot-tall cuckoo bird makes its presence known. Inside the clock a shop sells clocks, Hummels, and other old-world gifts. (615) 453–0414.

At Carbo's Police Museum, along the Parkway, you'll see the 1974 Corvette in which Tennessee's *Walking Tall* sheriff, Buford Pusser, was killed. (For more on Buford Pusser, see the McNairy County entries in chapter 5, The Western Plains.) Also at Carbo's are displays featuring police badges, uniforms, weapons, and other police items from around the world.

Applewood Farms is located just off Route 441 at 230 Lonesome Valley Road, right where Pigeon Forge and Sevierville meet. A working apple orchard, the barn was converted into a cider mill in 1981, just in time to attract people from forty-five different states and ten foreign countries who were in the area visiting the 1982 World's Fair in nearby Knoxville. Owners Bill Kilpatrick and Bon Hicks knew they had something going and started to expand.

Today, in addition to the cider mill, they have a bakery, a candy factory, a smokehouse, and a gift shop featuring crafts, gifts, and souvenir items. In 1987 their old farmhouse home was turned into the Applewood Farmhouse Restaurant. On the menu you'll find traditional items such as prime rib and steaks, but you'll also find local favorites, including fried biscuits and fresh Smoky Mountain trout. One of the favorites is trout cake, made from crumbled trout mixed with cheese and onions. But save room for some wonderful apple dessert. The homemade apple pies are always a favorite, but the apple fritters, accompanied by home-made apple butter, are also high on the list for apple lovers. Open daily; (615) 453–9319.

About 4 miles north on Route 441, or the Dolly Parton Parkway as they call it around here, is the downtown section of Dolly's hometown, Sevierville. Stop and ask about her and you'll be amazed at how many "good friends" this lady has. Less commercial than the other communities along Route 441, the downtown section has retained most of its small, mountain atmosphere. In a walking tour of twenty-six historic landmarks, you'll get to see a bronze, life-size statue of Dolly.

Knox County

Heading to Knoxville from Sevierville on Highway 441/411, you'll pass an abundance of antique and craft shops, potteries, and souvenir and gift shops. When the highways split, continue on Highway 441 into Knoxville until you cross the Tennessee River. That big golden ball you see high in the air to your left as you cross the river is the **Sunsphere,** the 300-foot-tall centerpiece of the 1982 World's Fair.

The Knoxville Arts Council now calls it home, but for a small fee, visitors can ride to the top and survey the fair site and the downtown section of the city. The adjacent amphitheater and parklike settings are used several times during the year for festivals, concerts, and all sorts of arts-related activities. (615) 523–2316.

Adjacent to the fair site is an area known as the 11th Avenue Artists' Colony. All four floors of the restored 1910 Candy Factory building and a row of Victorian houses behind it house various galleries and art workshops. The Knoxville Museum of Art is located in the factory building while its new $10 million home is being built next door. Products available to the public to purchase range from ceramic mugs to textile hangings. This entire colony has the most fine art available in a small area in the entire state.

Down the hill from the World's Fair site is the main campus of the University of Tennessee, where the Volunteers play their football games in the 95,000-plus-seat Neyland Stadium. It's only natural that tailgate partiers would adapt to the unique position of the stadium next to the Tennessee River. The Volunteer Navy, as it is called, starts gathering as early as Thursday before a Saturday game, and by game time as many as 300 boats have tied up. The only traffic these folks have to contend with is walking across the street to the stadium. Washington State is the only other major college stadium in the nation accessible by water.

Colorful "Big Orange" football is king in the fall, but the pinks and whites of flowering dogwoods dominate the city's attention each spring. City officials estimate that about a million such trees bloom in their city each year. A Dogwood Arts Festival is held annually during late April with arts, crafts, and other activities. There are six designated "dogwood trails" in the city for self-guided tours. Free bus tours leave hourly from the festival grounds at Market Square Mall.

East of Knoxville on Campbell Station Road, just off busy Route 11 in Farragut, among the commercial clutter of a typical suburban area rests an oasis of country style. The Appalachian Log Square is a showcase for the Appalachian Log Homes company, but it is also a unique shopping area. Containing six upscale country shops, a few offices, and the Apple Cake Tea Room restaurant, the complex not only shows off the workmanship of the log home company, but it also brings in money at the same time and provides a peaceful setting for a few shopkeepers. The tea room is a very country oriented eatery that specializes in soups, sandwiches, and quiches. (615) 966–7848.

Blount County

Another example of the old-time company town is found along Highway 129, south of Knoxville. Incorporated in 1919, the city of Alcoa was created by the Aluminum Company of America (AL-COA). Corporate offices are in Pittsburgh, but the southern plant opened in 1913 in a town called North Maryville. Six years later, with the financial help of the corporation, the city was created and its name changed.

Sam Houston, Davy Crockett's good friend and commander at the Alamo, came to Blount County with his family when he was fourteen years of age and soon developed a fascination for the life-style of the neighboring Cherokee Indians. Soon he was adopted by the Cherokees, who called him "The Raven."

He left the Indians to take a teaching position in a one-room schoolhouse near Maryville. He had little formal education but had read every book he could get his hands on, had won every spelling contest he entered, and could recite large portions of Homer's *Iliad* from memory. His teaching career lasted one term. In March 1813, he gave up teaching to enlist in General Andrew Jackson's army to fight the Creek Indian War.

The schoolhouse where he taught still stands and is considered the oldest original schoolhouse in the state and the only building left having a close association with this famous soldier and statesman. Built in 1794, the school now houses many of Houston's artifacts, including a pair of lead knuckles with his name carved in the soft metal. Did he use them to keep order in the classroom? the guide speculates.

The site also includes a visitors center and museum exhibits. It's located 6 miles north of Maryville on Sam Houston Schoolhouse Road, off Highway 33. Open year-round; admission free; (615) 983–1550.

Before the Smoky Mountains became a national park in 1935, the little community of Townsend was a major lumbering center. The **Little River Railroad and Lumber Company,** headed by

Col. W. B. Townsend, set up mills and harvested logs from the rich, fertile forests that are now federal lands.

Today, very little of that heritage exists. Townsend is a gateway to the Smokies, and tourism is the major industry. In the center of town on Highway 321, the Smoky Junction Restaurant specializes in all-you-can-eat catfish dinners and homemade chicken and dumplings. Out back, the Little River Railroad and Lumber Company Museum features a restored Shay Engine No. 2147 that was used locally during the early 1900s.

A restored train depot serves as a museum that's filled with memorabilia and photos of early railroad and lumbering industries. Admission free; (615) 448–6366.

The Dogwood Mall, on Scenic Highway 73 near the Cades Cove entrance to the park, features a variety of shops specializing in handmade mountain items, crafts, and artwork. Such items as brooms, wooden toys, quilts, stained glass, and fine art and prints are available from more than thirty local artisans.

Farther along Scenic Highway 73 is the little River Pottery & Country Store. This is one shop that's not easy to miss or resist. On nice days, the owners line the front porch and lawn with rocking chairs and loom-woven coverlets. Inside, wheel-thrown pottery lines the walls. It's the kind of shop that beckons to you as you try to drive by.

Down the road a piece is the Strawberry Patch Inn where the front porch is covered with tools, toys, furniture, and other artifacts of the past.

Monroe County

Sequoyah was an uneducated, crippled Cherokee half-breed who was shunned by his peers for much of his life until, in 1821, he introduced an alphabet to his people. It was so easy to learn that soon thousands were using it. Before long the Cherokees were more literate than most of the white men living in the area.

Sequoyah is the only man to single-handedly develop and perfect an alphabet. In doing so, he endowed an entire nation with learning. The story of Sequoyah is told in the Sequoyah Birthplace Museum, located south of Vonore on Highway 360, owned and operated by the Cherokee people.

The museum is dedicated to the brilliant Indian, but it also tells a great deal about the Cherokee Indians as a nation. Displays range from Indian artifacts to a present-day Blondie comic book written in the Cherokee alphabet. An adjacent gift shop offers a wide variety of Cherokee crafts, works of art, and related books. (615) 884–6246.

Along Highway 68, just outside of Sweetwater, you'll find something quite amazing "under the beaten path." It's the **Lost Sea,** an attraction the Guinness Book of World Records calls the "world's largest underground lake." It's a four-and-a-half-acre "bottomless" lake, 300 feet underground.

The fifty-five-minute tour is an easy walk down to the lake. There's not a single step to concern yourself with, since all paths are sloping, with handrails. Glass-bottomed boats take you out onto the lake, and white trout will gather around the boat as you approach their end of the lake. The tour guides are local and have quite a few interesting stories to tell. They might even try to scare you a few times as you walk along. Make sure you ask about the cave's nightclub, complete with a wooden dance floor.

Lost Sea has been designated as a Registered Natural Landmark by the U. S. Department of the Interior because of the lake phenomenon and the abundance of rare crystalline formations throughout the cavern system. Open year-round; (615) 337–6616.

The people of the Coker Creek area are still shouting, "There's gold in them thar hills!" The community has been celebrating the Autumn Gold Festival each October since 1968 to highlight the area's two forms of gold—the golden color of the leaves as they turn each fall and the gold that can still be found in the creeks of the area. The festival salutes the gold-mining heritage of the region, which goes back to the late 1820s.

Harold Witt brings down a few truckloads of dirt each year from his mountain gold mine so festival-goers have a better chance of finding some real gold when they participate in one of the major events, panning for gold. There are also turkey shoots, board splitting, syrup making, gospel and country music, and arts and crafts.

Coker Creek is located on Highway 68 a few miles from North Carolina in the Cherokee National Forest area. Downtown consists of the post office in Mamie Murphy's house. She's the postmistress and ran the postal business out of the general store until 1988 when it burned down.

The festival is held at Coker Creek Village, a family resort area a few miles out of town. At that facility, a big general store type of building has been constructed and now houses Coker Creek

Crafts, a basket business owned by Ken and Kathleen Dalton. Their quality baskets are in craft collections and museums all over the country. They do some work here, but most of it is done in their home workshop nearby. (615) 261–2157.

Loudon County

The **Crosseyed Cricket** advertises that it's more than "just a place to stay." Located on Paw Paw Road a few miles from Exit 364 on Interstate 40, about 20 miles southwest of Knoxville, the Cricket is a restaurant–public fishing–camping complex in a beautiful rural setting.

The restaurant is located in a 150-year-old operating gristmill and an adjacent 50-year-old log cabin overlooking the lake. The specialties are rainbow trout and channel catfish, both caught and cleaned fresh every day from the lake. Hush puppies, cole-slaw, and homemade pies round out the menu.

There are two fish-out lakes, one for the trout and one for the catfish. Public fishing is allowed, and you pay by the pound for what you catch. They'll provide everything you need, including bait, for free if you didn't bring your own. If you wish, they'll clean your catch and send it over to the restaurant, where it will be cooked to your taste. Otherwise, they'll pack it on ice and you can take it home with you. There are forty-seven campsites on the far side of the lake. There's no need to have a fishing license either; they have one that covers anyone who fishes their lakes. Open year-round; (615) 986–5435.

Roane County

The county is dominated by the Tennessee Valley Authority's (TVA) Watts Bar Lake. With 783 miles of lakefront, water-oriented activities are quite popular. Numerous marinas with boat rentals are scattered throughout the county. Once on the lake, island hopping is a popular activity. Hundreds of small islands make perfect secluded areas for picnicking and swimming.

Watts Bar Lake is one of several TVA lakes throughout the state that make up the chain called the "The Great Lakes of the South." Many families live on the lake in houseboats. One colony is located just west of Kingston off Highway 70.

The TVA steam plant in Kingston has free tours. There's no way you can miss it; just follow the roads to the big stacks. Elsewhere, a driving tour of the county has been developed, as has a backcountry trail driving tour. Brochures and maps for both are available from the Tourism Center, 339 West Race Street, Kingston; (615) 376–5572.

Morgan County

Dot Byrd is a celebrity in the Back Valley area, near Coalfield. She has the distinction of operating the **World's Smallest Library.** She's been on the "Johnny Carson Show," and film crews from throughout the world have found the Back Valley Public Library, located in the front yard of her and husband Samuel's home. In 1989 she was the grand marshal of Coalfield High School's homecoming parade.

Once a month the county's bookmobile comes out and re-stocks the library with about 1,000 titles. The 5-foot by 6-foot library is officially open every Tuesday from 3:30 to 7:30 P.M.

Dot has lived in the same house for the past thirty-three years and knows most of the several hundred people who live in the area that her library serves. The small building is centered in a well-kept flower garden and is never locked. "The dogs usually let us know when someone comes in," Samuel said. The library is located about 4 miles from Oliver Springs off Highway 62 on Back Valley Road. (615) 435–7819.

If it's rugged wilderness and wild white water you're looking for, follow Highway 27 north to Wartburg and the Obed Wild and Scenic River. The area is managed by the National Park Service and the Tennessee Wildlife Resources Agency and consists of four streams within the same watershed. Through the years, they have carved their way through the landscape and have created beautiful gorges, some as deep as 500 feet.

During the rainy season, from December through April, the streams provide some of the finest, most technical white water in the nation. Some primitive camping is allowed. The visitors center for the area is in the Federal Building in Wartburg. (615) 346–6294.

Of the three utopian experiments in Tennessee during the late 1800s, Rugby's was the largest and has left us with the most evidence of the dreamers' struggles. (See the Ruskin Cave entry for Dickson County, in the Heartland section of this book, for information on another utopian colony.)

World's Smallest Library

Today, seventeen of the seventy original buildings of **Rugby's Utopian Community** still stand and have been preserved or restored. Many are still inhabited by descendants of the original settlers.

In 1880, English author-reformer Thomas Hughes launched this colony with the dream that it would be "a centre in which a healthy, reverent life shall grow." At its peak in 1884, population was about 450. Today, Rugby has about seventy residents.

Hughes' vision of a utopian existence in the wilderness of Tennessee brought a taste of British culture along with it. Most of the settlers were young British aristocrats, and today their colorful Victorian legacies line the streets, making Rugby one of the most unusual communities in the state.

A journey through town should begin at the old Rugby Schoolhouse, which now serves as a museum and visitors center. In addition to the school, historic buildings open to visitors include the Christ Church, Episcopal, with its original hanging lamps and 1849 rosewood reed organ; Kingstone Lisle, the restored home built for Hughes; and the Thomas Hughes Free Public Library, which still contains what is regarded as the greatest collection (7,000 volumes) of Victorian literature in America.

Two historic structures have been restored and now offer overnight accommodations with historic accuracy. The Pioneer Cottage and the Newbury House Inn are available with prior reservations. Several other early structures house gift shops and restaurants.

If you're into ghosts and stories of haunting, you'll get your fill during your tour of Rugby's historic district. If your guide doesn't talk about the various sightings through the years, make sure you ask. Rugby is located on Route 52, a few miles west of Highway 27. Structures are open daily, March through mid-December. Housing, shops, and restaurants are open year-round. (615) 628–2441.

Anderson County

In 1942, as World War II was raging, President Franklin D. Roosevelt approved the proposal by Albert Einstein to proceed in making a secret weapon. The Army Corps of Engineers chose an isolated 60,000-acre site here in Anderson County; within one year, three defense plants were built and a **"Secret City"** of 75,000 was cut out of the wilderness.

Throughout the war years, Oak Ridge, the name given the

community, remained under direct supervision of the government and was surrounded by a tall barbed-wire fence. Only a handful of the workers knew the true nature of the project, and all were sworn to secrecy. It was not until the dropping of the first atomic bombs in 1945 that the inhabitants behind the fences learned that they had been members of an important team of the famed Manhattan Project. Oak Ridge produced the uranium 235 and plutonium 239, the fuel necessary for the atomic bomb.

The fences went down in 1949, and the city was incorporated. Today, most of that original "top secret" community exists. All three plants are still there, but the main emphasis in Oak Ridge now is energy research.

The original graphite reactor, which was the first full producing nuclear reactor in the world, is open to the public and is located in the X-10 (every location has a code name) building. A map of the 38-mile self-guided motor tour of the entire area is available at the visitors center, 300 S. Tulane Ave.; (615) 482–7821.

Next to the visitors center, the U.S. Department of Energy has developed one of the world's largest energy exhibitions. The **American Museum of Science and Energy** includes interactive exhibits, live demonstrations, computer displays, and filmed interpretations. All forms of energy and their relationship to humanity are explained. One favorite demonstration, especially of the young, makes a person's hair stand straight up on end. Admission free; (615) 576–3200.

The story behind the creation of the living areas of Oak Ridge is quite an amazing one. Five home designs were created and assigned to workers according to family size and job importance. Neighborhoods centered on the Town Site, which was designed to offer shopping and recreation. The high school, multifamily housing, and the hospital were also built near the Town Site. Now known as Jackson Square, a walking-tour map of that original town site is available.

West of Oak Ridge, on Highway 62, the University of Tennessee has established a forestry experiment station. The arboretum is open to the public and has three designated nature walking tours. More than 800 species of plants grow here naturally, and most of them are labeled for easy identification by visitors. Specific information about the experimental work being done at any particular time is available at the visitors center. (615) 483–3571.

On Highway 61 in downtown Clinton, The Twins Cafe at 363 Market Street is open six days a week from 4:00 A.M. to 4:00 P.M. Twins Hassie and Lassie have owned the establishment since

1953 and have "no desire to retire." In 1989, at age eighty-eight, Hassie went to the doctor for a checkup. "He told me I was good for at least another eighty-eight years," she said. "Then he came over and had some of our biscuits and gravy."

Up at 4:00 A.M. to make fresh biscuits and pies, the two wait on tables as well as prepare the meals. One other waitress is on duty during the busy periods. Hassie said it really isn't hard work. "We pretty much know what each person wants, and when we see them come through the front door, we get it ready. If I'm not friends with a person when they come in, I will be by the time they leave," she predicted. Closed on Sunday; (615) 457–9970.

The Community Crafts Center and Shop is located on Highway 61 about a mile after it crosses Interstate 75. The center was started in 1970 to "enrich the souls and pocketbooks of low-income people." Today, the nonprofit organization that runs the center works with local people to preserve traditional Appalachian crafts and techniques. All types of crafts are available.

About a mile down the road from the crafts center is the **Museum of Appalachia.** Founded by John Rice Irwin in 1960, the museum is considered one of the most authentic representations of early Appalachian mountain life. Dozens of cabins and buildings have been moved here and preserved in the spaciousness of their original locations. More than 250,000 items are on display. Live music and demonstrations abound as employees go about living and working in a mountain village. *Roots* author Alex Haley said he loved the museum so much that he "built a home in sight of it." He lives directly next door. (615) 494–7680.

The nearby city of Norris is a great little community. Planned and built by the Tennessee Valley Authority (TVA) in 1934 as a demonstration of sound community development, the town features a green belt; a town forest, which protects the city's water supply; and houses placed in a parklike atmosphere. Now an independent municipality, Norris has preserved its original look. Brochures and information are available at the police and fire departments.

The Tennessee Valley Authority act was signed into law by President Franklin Roosevelt on May 18, 1933, and within a few weeks, the TVA's first flood-control project, the Norris Dam, was started. As the oldest TVA facility, the dam is open to visitors on occasion, although the entire operation is now run by remote control.

The dam and the lake make up a part of the Norris Dam State

Park, as does the **Lenoir Family Museum.** Made up primarily of Will G. Lenoir's "junk" collection, items in the state-run facility date from prehistoric times to the present. The place is filled with artifacts that visitors are encouraged to pick up and touch. As the guides walk visitors through, they tell stories that bring the items to life. Many of the stories are more fun than the items themselves. To get the full benefit here, take the tour first and listen to the stories, then go back through and look at the displays at your own pace.

The museum's most treasured artifact is a European barrel organ with tiers of hand-carved wooden figures. It has been completely restored, and a free concert is given each Saturday at 10:30 A.M. Research shows it was made in Germany in 1826 and probably brought to America by a traveling showman. Admission free; (615) 494–9688.

Outside, the TVA has gathered two additional buildings. The Cosby Threshing Barn, built in the early 1800s, was one of the first threshing barns to be built in the U.S. It's full of pioneer machinery, including a wooden treadmill made in 1855. Across the field from the barn is a 1798 gristmill where corn is ground during the summer months. A gift shop is on the upper level. The entire setting is very rustic and just a short distance from the dam and a picnic area.

There are several caves within the park, but only one is open to the public. A tour of Hill Cave which can be reached only by boat, is led by a park naturalist. The cave features many formations and is not equipped to handle large crowds, unlike nearby commercial caves. A few safety devices have been added, but the rest is as wild as it was when discovered. (615) 426–7461.

Campbell County

The 667-acre Cove Lake State Recreational Area is located on the banks of Cove Lake, near Caryville. Established in the 1930s as a recreation demonstration area by the TVA, the National Park Service, and the Civilian Conservation Corps, the lake is home to more than 400 Canada geese each winter. Surrounded by the towering Cumberland Mountains, the park is perhaps more popular with vistors in the winter than the summer. Attracted by the quiet inlets, marshes, and fields of the area, the geese come in late fall and stay through early spring. To supplement the wild food and attract geese into view, rangers put out corn near the Cove Lake Restaurant, which has a full menu of country cooking favorites and seats about 115. Open daily year-round.

The restaurant and the ranger's station and the masonry fences around them were built by the Civilian Conservation Corps.

Christmas in the Park is an annual event that county residents look forward to. The celebration features all sorts of music, lights, and decorations throughout the park. The walkways and roads are lined with candles. In the summer, the park offers an Olympic-size swimming pool open to the public. (615) 562–8355.

Scott County

This entire county has been described by many as one big natural museum. *Ruggedness* is the key word here, and one access to that ruggedness is through the **Big South Fork National River and Recreation Area.**

Authorized by Congress in 1974, the park has been frequented mainly by those who have been willing to explore the wilderness on its own terms. During the last few years, more roads, overlooks, and river access sites have been built, opening up the 100,000-acre park to less adventurous visitors.

The Big South Fork River cuts a course through one of the most spectacular chasms east of the Mississippi. The gorge is rimmed by towering bluffs of weathered sandstone, rising as high as 500 feet. It's considered to be one of the best white-water rivers in the East. In all, there are more than 80 miles of prime canoeing waters within the park.

Camping is permitted just about anywhere in the park, and mountain bikes and fourwheeled off-road vehicles are permitted on designated trails and roads. There are three developed campgrounds and the Charit Creek Hotel, dormitory style housing with bunk beds. There is no electricity here and no vehicular traffic is allowed. (615) 569–6900.

The most comfortable way to see the rugged terrain and the river is aboard the Big South Fork Scenic Railway. The three-hour narrated trip leaves from the historic coal-mining town of Stearns, Kentucky. The 11-mile trip takes you down gently to the bottom of the gorge, through a massive tunnel, and along high rock ledges. It then hugs the banks of the river, where you might catch a glimpse of white-water aficionados. (800) 462–5664.

Off the Beaten Path along the Plateaus and Valleys

1. Alvin York State Historic Area
2. Beggar's Castle
3. Court Square Emporium
4. Talavera De La Reina
5. Homesteads
6. Rhea County Courthouse
7. Washington Ferry
8. Spit and Whittle Gang
9. McMinn County Living Heritage Museum
10. Tennessee's Badlands
11. Ocoee Flume
12. Cherokee National Forest
13. Primitive Settlement
14. Red Clay
15. Last Battle of the Revolution
16. Chattanooga Choo Choo
17. TVA's Raccoon Mountain Pumped Storage Facility
18. Riverside Catfish House
19. Dutch Maid Bakery
20. Wonder Cave
21. Old Wood Village
22. Rivendell Farm
23. Coke Ovens Historic Site
24. Cumberland Caverns
25. Harold's Place
26. H & H Pig Farm
27. Cookeville Depot Museum
28. OshKosh B'Gosh
29. Red Boiling Springs

Plateaus & Valleys

Fentress County

In a valley surrounded by the Cumberland Mountains a few miles from the Kentucky border, Sergeant Alvin York, one of America's most celebrated military heroes, was born and reared. Except for the two years he spent in the war, Sergeant York spent his entire life in these mountains. But those two years put York in the history books and this part of the state on the map. Today, the **Alvin York State Historic Area** commemorates his life and career.

York's one-man firefight with the German Army in France's Argonne Forest on October 8, 1918, is now legendary. As a patrol leader, he killed 25 German soldiers and almost single-handedly captured another 132. As a result, he received more than forty Allied decorations and worldwide publicity.

His modest upbringing here in the Tennessee mountains and his refusal to cash in on his popularity by selling out to the media won the hearts of millions, and he returned to the valley as a bona fide hero.

York died in 1964, and four years later the state bought a large portion of land that included his family farm and the mill that he once operated. The exhibits are fine, but the real reason to visit this area is the park ranger, York's son, Andy York. He'll be more than glad to spend some time with you and tell you all sorts of stories about his famous father and the family's ties to the area. It's not too often that you get to meet a genuine hero's son whose business it is to talk about his father's life. It's a unique opportunity to put history into perspective.

The area is about 7 miles north of Jamestown on Highway 127; open daily; (615) 879–9948.

While you're in the area, plan a little adventure for lunch time: eat at the **Beggar's Castle** restaurant. The food is great and the atmosphere unique. Located about 4 miles south of Jamestown, off Highway 127, Roger Salomon's establishment is truly off the beaten path. In fact, it might be wise when you call for reservations to ask for specific directions.

Salomon was born in Germany and came from a family that has operated restaurants and inns for the past 400 years. He makes his own sausages and cures his own ham, bakes his own breads, and makes his own creams and mayonnaise. The local farmers raise his pork, veal, vegetables, and herbs.

One of the best items here is the German meat pie, made with pork, chicken breast, veal, and three types of cheeses. Other specialites include the daily veal and chicken specials. Entree prices go up to $14.95. Closed Mondays; (615) 879–8993.

After you eat, go back out to Highway 127 and turn south. About a mile down the road is the Highland Manor Winery, which has the distinction of being the first licensed winery in the state and the first American winery to be awarded the International Gold Medal for Quality in Madrid, Spain. Currently, this is one of the eleven commercial wineries in the state. (See Grundy County later in this section and Montgomery County in the Heartlands section for additional fruit-of-the-vine experiences.) Open Monday through Saturday for tours and tasting; (615) 879–9519.

Overton County

In the heart of the Upper Cumberland region, Livingston, the county seat, is rapidly becoming known for its quality crafts outlets. The downtown area around the historic courthouse is known as Court Square and is the home of many retail shops, antique stores, and crafts stores.

The largest of these is the 6,000-square-foot **Court Square Emporium.** With a minimum of thirty exhibitors at any one time, the place represents a major home-based manufacturing concern that produces one-of-a-kind local products.

As renovation of the square area continues, current shop owners are optimistic that more establishments will be opened, making the area a stronger draw for those searching for Tennessee mountain crafts. Currently most of the stores are open daily except Sunday.

With a state as full of outdoor recreational facilities as Tennessee, it's difficult to call one facility unique, but the Bend of the River Shooting Center could well be. Located on Highway 136 about 6 miles south of Hilham, in the county's southwest section, the 100-acre center offers pistol and archery shooting ranges, a high-power–rifle range, and skeet and trap fields. In the rustic lodge, a variety of classes in shooting and firearm safety are held.

Owner Charlie Pardue welcomes shooters, "wanna-be" shooters, and spectators. If you don't have any weapons with you, you can rent a bow or gun for $3 a day, and shoot all you want for an additional $4. Ammunition is extra, of course. It's free if you just want to watch, and Charlie will lend you a pair of ear protectors. Open Saturdays only; (615) 498–2829.

On your way to Cumberland County, make sure you drive through Overton's small Mennonite community in Muddy Pond. Off Highway 164, in the deep Southeast portion of the county, you'll be able to watch true craftsmen create fine horse-drawn buggies and wagons and the harnesses and saddles to go with them. Several homes along the rural routes sell breads, pies, and eggs. Just look for the signs and stop by. If you buy a few products, chances are the people will be happy to tell you about their peaceful lives in this almost hidden community.

Cumberland County

Amy Brissler, owner of **Talavera De La Reina** (Tavern of the Queen), the most unusual eatery in this county, was born and raised in rural Overton County, went to Hollywood in 1935, and mingled with the stars for about forty years. When she decided it was time to come home, she retired to the land she owned out "in the wilds of Tennessee."

On that land she started to build the restaurant of her dreams piece by piece, as money would allow. In fact, that piecemeal approach is one of the factors that makes this establishment unique. She got the walls up, but superstar Marie McDonald had to supply the money to put the roof on.

Although the food is excellent, it's only part of the dining experience. Brissler, known around here as "the Queen," was one of the best costume designers in the film and television industries. Some of her creations, including dresses made for Mae West, Marilyn Monroe, Judy Garland, and a cape she made for Liberace, hang in the restaurant. She worked on one of the gowns worn by Viven Leigh in *Gone With the Wind,* and a replica of that dress, made from the original bolt of material, is also on display.

Memorabilia, sketches from her own work, and autographed photos line the walls, and a portrait that Brissler painted of her friend Mae West hangs over the bar.

Talavera is officially a private club, but is open for lunch and dinner to the public with advance reservations. To find the Queen's kingdom, go out Interstate 40, west of Crossville, to exit

311. Go 1 mile south on Plateau Road; then 1 mile west on Highway 70; then 3 miles north on Jim Garrett Road. (615) 277–3749.

South of Crossville, where Highways 127 and 68 split, is the planned community of **Homesteads.** The area, with its quaint little stone houses lining both highways, is often referred to as the "showplace of the New Deal."

In January 1934, following several years of hard times in the area, the local farm agent submitted an application to the government for one of the subsistence projects formulated by the Roosevelt administration. The application was accepted and work began on the 10,000-acre project.

The plan was to build 250 homesteads, each of about twenty acres. The homesteaders were selected following a series of intense background checks and interviews of about 4,000 applicants. Cooperatives were established for the community, and family members went to these to make their family's mattresses, can their family's food, or weave at a loom house.

Today, most of the homes are still standing and can be seen from atop the 80-foot-tall octagonal tower that originally served as a water tower for the community. At the base is a sandstone building, which housed the administrative offices of the project. Today those offices serve as a museum depicting Roosevelt's homesteading project. If you want, you can climb the ninety-seven steps to the top of the tower.

Of the 102 New Deal projects, the Cumberland Homesteads was considered one of the most, if not the most, successful of all. Admission to the museum and art gallery is free, but if you climb the tower, it will cost you 50 cents. Open daily except Tuesday and Wednesday; (615) 484–2697.

In addition to the museum, tower, and original homesteads, the area also has two interesting country stores, right next to each other, and across the street from the tower. Claiming to sell "Goods in Endless Variety for Man & Beast," the Cumberland General store specializes in new old-fashioned items for the modern-day homesteader. One of the best areas of the store, however, is a book section that sells how-to-books on such lost arts as hog butchering, building a stone fence, and hand digging a well. Open daily; (615) 484–8481.

Next door in a ramshackle old building is the Homestead Country Store. Talk about an eclectic inventory! From the wooden rockers on the porch to the antiques, reproductions, and food and craft items inside, the store will keep you busy for quite some

The New Deal Homesteads Tower

time if you're a real bargain hunter. You aren't a shopper? Well, while your traveling companion snoops around inside, buy a can of pop and rest yourself in a rocking chair out front and watch the world go by. You'll have just as much fun! Open daily; (615) 484–2760.

Rhea County

It's hard to believe that Dayton, a small city just north of Chattanooga, was probably a household world from coast to coast during the long, hot summer of 1925. That's when the silver-tongued orators, William Jennings Bryan and Clarence Darrow, engaged in a legal battle in the **Rhea County Courthouse.** The Scopes "Monkey Trial" let the world know that a Dayton outside of Ohio actually did exist. Although John Scopes, a schoolteacher, didn't reach the heights that the Wright Brothers of the other Dayton did, he earned himself a place in history.

The courthouse has been restored to its 1925 vintage and now houses a small museum in its basement. There you'll find newspaper clippings, photos, and actual newsreel footage of what many still call the first major trial treated as a media event.

Scopes was accused of teaching the Darwinian theory of evolution to a high school biology class in violation of a recently passed Tennessee statute making it unlawful "to teach any theory that denies the story of the divine creation of man as taught in the Bible."

Scopes wasn't even the school's regular biology teacher, but a math teacher filling in. He was fined $100, a fee he never paid. Open Monday through Saturday; admission free; (615) 775–0817.

To get to Meigs County, follow Highway 30 out of Dayton until it disappears into the Tennessee River. If you're lucky, your timing will get you there as the **Washington Ferry** is loading. If not, there's never much of a wait.

In operation since 1803, the $1/3$-mile trek across the river is the third-oldest operating ferry route in the U.S. There has been a major debate in the area since about 1927 as to where to build a bridge. "Until they figure out where to build that bridge, we'll be in business," said ferry owner Charles Smith. There's another ferry about 10 miles downriver on Highway 60.

The eight-car boat takes about ten minutes to cross the river and costs $2 per vehicle. If you have to wait, take a minute and ask the fishermen at the ferry slip how the fish are biting. You may end up in a conversation that will be so interesting that you won't mind if you miss your boat. There's no night operation across the river, and it operates year-round.

Meigs County

Continue on Highway 30, and you'll come to the small county seat community of Decatur where a historic town square will attract your attention. Unlike many of the older courthouse squares, this one is a bit barren and free of large trees.

But in the shadow of the courthouse, you'll find the area's version of the **Spit and Whittle Gang,** a bunch of old-timers who gather each day to—well, you guessed it.

Over behind the post office, you'll find an old law office building that was built in the early 1900s. The same lawyer who purchased the building in 1948 to set up his practice still runs it there today. His front door sign reads: "Open when I get here. Closed when I get tired."

McMinn County

In Athens, just off Highway 30, rests Tennessee Wesleyan College, a liberal arts school established in 1857. The first building on campus, appropriately called the "Old College" building, is still standing and up until 1989 housed the county's heritage museum.

The structure, built in 1854 and also used as a hospital during the Civil War, faces the quad grounds of the school. Behind Old College, on Dwain Farmer Drive, you'll find a marker explaining one of the most poignant legends in Tennessee history.

A wounded English officer from nearby Fort Loudon was befriended by an Indian chief and nursed back to health by Nocatula, daughter of the chief. The soldier, given the name of Connestoga (the oak), was accepted into the tribe and married Nocatula. A jealous suitor attacked Connestoga with a knife. As he lay dying, Nocatula confessed her eternal love and plunged a knife into her breast.

The pair were buried together, and the chief placed an acorn in Connestoga's hand and a hackberry in Nocatula's hand, symbolizing undying love. From these there developed two trees that grew intertwined on this spot for more than 150 years.

After these two original trees died in 1957, two others were planted. Those have since died, and today the stumps are all that remain.

The **McMinn County Living Heritage Museum** moved out of the Old College building in late 1989 and moved to the city's old high school gymnasium building, about a half-mile from downtown, on Madison Street.

The museum's collection of nineteenth- and twentieth-century quilts is one of the finest in the state. In addition to the permanent display of quilts, a nationally known quilt show is hosted by the museum each February.

In addition, there is also a great children's collection that includes china and bisque-head dolls, toys, and clothing, along with school desks, books and maps dating from 1850. Admission is charged; open daily except Mondays and major holidays; (615) 745–0329.

Polk County

If you happen to be in this part of the state and are tired of beautiful, lush mountains and forests, trek on over to the Ducktown area, a portion of the state often referred to as **Tennessee's Badlands.**

Here you won't be surrounded by lush, green vegetation. In fact, you'll be surrounded by a 56-square-mile area of barren red hills, stunted pine trees, and washed-out gullies. This area of raw landscape is similar in looks to the famed badlands areas of the Dakotas.

Geographically, the area is known as the Copper Basin and was the site of a thriving copper-mining industry that lasted 144 years, ending on July 31, 1987.

Intensive reforestation has made a big dent in the destruction, but in 1978 local residents made a move to put an end to the reforestation efforts and to preserve the area as a unique part of Tennessee's history. Today, the Ducktown Basin Museum has been opened to not only preserve various artifacts and memorabilia of the mining operations but also educate people about what went on in this corner of the state.

The museum is located on thirteen acres of the former Burra

Burra Mine site, now a national designated historic district, in the community of Ducktown, just off Highway 64. It was organized in 1983 and has been "run on a shoestring" ever since, according to Bobbie Jean Beckler, a leader of the movement to preserve the basin area.

Inside the museum you'll find a great many photos, maps, copper ore samples, and the various tools of the trade. Since the total demise of the industry was predated by efforts to preserve it, a true, complete representation of the area is on display, or soon will be. You'll also have a pretty good shot at meeting one of the people who worked the mines, who will be able to give you a first-hand account of the operation.

Jim Cole, whose family worked in the area for generations, is an accomplished carver, and his work, depicting people working the tasks of the industry, are on display in the museum. These carvings are great examples of Tennessee folk art.

Tours are given through the various Burra Burra buildings every day, except Sundays during the winter. If you want to see a part of Tennessee that most of the state's residents don't even know exists, here's your chance. It has to be the most overlooked, historically significant area in the entire state. Admission is charged; (615) 496–5778.

Farther down Highway 64, between Ducktown and Cleveland, you'll find yourself driving along the Ocoee River, one of the top ten white-water rivers in the country. You'll also find numerous business establishments that will be more than happy to rent you a raft, canoe, or kayak so you too can experience an adventure of a lifetime.

If you're not of the adventurous variety or don't have the time, there are several pull-offs where you can experience the dangers and the excitement vicariously. The mostly two-lane road is very busy here, so be careful to pull off the road completely before looking too much.

Look closely through the trees on the other side of the river and you'll see the largest wooden flume known to exist in the United States. The **Ocoee Flume** is 5 miles long, 11 feet wide and 14 feet tall. Originally built in 1912 by the Tennessee Valley Authority (TVA), it was closed for a few years in the late 1970s and was rebuilt.

Its major function is to divert water from the river to help produce hydroelectric power, but recently it has also been a savior of the river for the white-water aficionados. With the diversion the flume creates, the TVA can produce their power and the river can still run to the point of whiteness.

Bradley County

Mention mountain forests and fantastic views, and most people think of the Smoky Mountains. That's why the 620,000-acre **Cherokee National Forest** here in the southeast portion of the state remains virtually untouched by crowds.

More than 1,100 miles of roads have been cut through the dense forest, opening up all sorts of opportunities for outdoor enthusiasts or for those who simply enjoy driving and looking. Take your time; there's a real good chance that no one will be honking and trying to get around you. The Forest Service maintains twenty-nine camping areas, horse trails (bring your own horse), and 105 hiking trails. This area is every bit as beautiful as the Smokies, making it a great alternative that most locals are hesitant to tell too many people about. The supervisor's office can give you more specifics; (615) 476–9700.

About 6 miles outside Cleveland on Highway 64E, hidden behind the hustle and bustle of a busy highway and a myriad of antique shops and flea markets, is a neat little living-history museum called the **Primitive Settlement.** Here, a collection of nineteenth-century log cabins from the area have been moved and rebuilt to show life the way it was. The owners claim that they have the area's largest collection of primitive antiques.

When you enter the gates, the settlement appears to be a small attraction, but once you start talking with the employees and sticking your head into the various corners, a visit can turn into a very interesting couple of hours. Each cabin, with the oldest being more than 150 years old, depicts a different mode of frontier life.

During the summer, live country music is offered every Saturday night. Open daily March through October; admission is charged; (615) 476–5096.

About 12 miles south of Cleveland, off a series of back roads, you'll find the historic **Red Clay** area. Red Clay was the site of the last council ground of the Cherokee Indian nation before their forced removal in 1838. It was the site of eleven general councils, national affairs attended by up to 5,000 Indians each.

The U.S. government wanted the Cherokees to surrender their

47

eastern lands and move the entire tribe to lands in Oklahoma. The Cherokees fought it for quite a while, but controversial treaties resulted in their losing the land. Here at Red Clay, the journey to Oklahoma, known today as the Trail of Tears, actually began.

The march, often referred to as the Great Removal, was a wintertime, cross-country journey that covered more than 1,000 miles. Reportedly, 4,000 of the 18,000 who were forced to leave perished during the walk. That was almost one-fourth of the entire Cherokee nation.

Today, people can drive that same path across the state on the "Trail of Tears State Historic Route." It's marked quite well, and maps that explain the various historical activities along the way are available here at Red Clay. About 80 percent of the original trail is now covered by modern highways.

Here where it all began a 275-acre state historic area has been developed. The only original part left is the council spring, locally known as the blue hole. It was this pure running spring that probably attracted the Cherokees to this site in the first place.

Also on the grounds are various reproductions of early Indian homesteads and an interpretive center with displays and historical exhibits.

It's not an easy place to find. Take Highway 60 south out of Cleveland and follow the signs. They are good signs but often understated in size and can be easily overlooked if you happen to be looking at the cows and horses along the way. If you see a sign that reads "Welcome to Georgia," you've gone about a half-mile too far. Open daily; admission free; (615) 472–2627.

Hamilton County

Chattanooga, the state's fourth largest city, with a population of less than 200,000, is located along a 7-mile bend in the Tennessee River. The deep ravine along the river is often referred to as the Grand Canyon of the South.

Lookout Mountain is probably the best known of the three major "ledges" that loom over the city. And, as in any major tourist destination, the beaten path and the unbeaten path catch up with each other here, with the same attraction often offering different things to different people.

Along with all its Civil War history, the area around Lookout Mountain contains a lesser-known fact about an earlier war. History books usually tell us that the American Revolution started at Lexington and ended with Cornwallis's surrender at Yorktown. Actually, historians currently say that the last engagement between official forces of the war took place on the slopes of Lookout Mountain on September 20, 1782, a year after Yorktown.

The National Park Service must agree with these historians, because they have marked the spot, just off Highway 148 near the foot of the mountain, with a historical marker, calling it the **"Last Battle of the Revolution."**

Farther up the mountain, one of the Civil War's most famous battles was fought. Known today as the "Battle Above the Clouds," the fight at Chickamauga Creek and the Battle of Chattanooga are immortalized in the nation's first and largest national military park. The huge park, established in 1890, contains more than 400 markers on the battlefield, outlining the series of events that claimed 34,000 casualties. In addition, the park also contains 666 monuments honoring the men who fought on the grounds.

The visitor center is a good place to start your education on the area's Civil War history. It's located on Highway 27.

As you climb the mountain, you'll pass several other well-known attractions, including the incredible Ruby Falls. They are very much on the beaten path but shouldn't be overlooked just because you don't like crowds or don't want to visit a place just because everyone else in the world has been there first.

Many Tennessee natives don't realize that one of the most popular attractions on Lookout Mountain, Rock City, is actually across the state line in Georgia.

"See Rock City" birdhouses and painted barn roofs throughout the Southeast have made this attraction a genuine piece of Americana. There's nothing like it anywhere else. Ten acres of natural rock gardens, some with formations looming twenty stories high, and a barren spot called Lover's Leap, where seven states can be seen, are the highlights of the attraction. Twisting paths take you through wonderfully landscaped gardens and narrow crevices. One such crack is thoughtfully named "Fat Man's Squeeze."

The founder, Garnet Carter, first built a hotel on the property and in early 1928 developed a recreational outlet that changed leisure-time activities from coast to coast. Using the natural hills, rocks, hollow logs, and pools of water as hazards, he created a miniature golf course for his guests who didn't want to take the time to play a complete round of regulation golf.

A Rock City Barn

Within a short time, various other hotels in the country asked him to design courses for them, and "Tom Thumb Golf" took the country by storm. By 1930 about 25,000 miniature golf courses were operating in the United States, many of which were Carter's courses.

The original course and the hotel are now gone, but several of the small characters that were placed around the course are now a part of the Fairyland portion of Rock City. Admission is charged; (404) 820–2531.

Less than a mile from Rock City, at the very top of the mountain, The Castle in the Clouds resort hotel was built in 1928. Today, the old hotel, since restored, is the main building for Covenant College, a small liberal arts school. Other buildings on the campus also have historical as well as nostalgic appeal. Drop by and look up one of the school's officials, who love to give tours. (404) 820–1560.

If you're a little leery about driving up the mountain, there's a solution. Built in 1895, the Lookout Mountain Incline is now a part of the city's transit system. Billed as the "World's Steepest and Safest Incline Railway," it has a 72.7-percent grade near the top. At the top of the mile-long ride, the upper station has been developed into a small retail village, which happens to have the best ice cream in the Chattanooga area. (615) 821–4224.

Pardon me boy, but let's go visit the **Chattanooga Choo Choo.** Down in the city, the Choo Choo is one of the most unusual shopping areas in the state. Located at the old Terminal Station, the complex features a Hilton Hotel with rooms in restored train cars, landscaped gardens, and a myriad of Victorian-era shops and restaurants. All play on the train theme.

The city was one of the country's earliest and largest railroad centers, and this station was the hub of that activity. On the top floor of one of the terminal buildings, one of the world's largest model railroad layouts has been created by a local model railroad club showing the area as it was during the heyday. During the week it can be seen running under automated control, but on weekends members of the club come out and "play" with their creation.

The entire display is 174 feet long and contains more than 3,000 square feet of space. The HO-gauge layout has about 100 locomotives and several hundred passenger and freight cars on about 100 miles of track. Admission charged.

Several stores sell 45-RPM records of Glen Miller's version of

Chattanooga Choo Choo

the Chattanooga Choo Choo song. The phrase itself was coined in 1880 when a reporter took the first train ride out of Cincinnati on the new Cincinnati-Southern Line. Since the tracks only went as far as this city, he called the train the "Chattanooga Choo Choo."

One shop to visit before you leave this complex is General Longstreet's Gallery. Original bullets and reproduction Confederate States ("CS") coat buttons and belt buckles are available, along with all kinds of other Civil War artifacts.

Also, for less than $10 you can buy enough soldiers (in blue and/or gray plastic) for 69 cents each to stage your own battles. Or you can buy a whole kit, which includes appropriate flags, for $2.95. This shop is also a good place to talk with some real experts about the area's Civil War heritage. These people live and breathe the Civil War. Be careful if you're a Yankee; some of those boys don't know the war is over.

Before leaving the city, another interesting stop is the National Knife Museum. Owned and operated by the National Knife Collectors Association, the new 8,000-square-foot museum was created to provide a showplace for the work of the association's 16,000 members. Private collections from members are on display, as is the museum's growing permanent collection. Handmade blades and knives from most of the 360 American cutlery firms are featured. By the way, one thing you'll find out here is

that a knife collector is technically known as a *machairologist.*
Admission free; (615) 899–9456.

Leave Chattanooga via Highway 41/64/72, also known as Will
Cummings Highway, toward Raccoon Mountain. As you approach the mountain, you'll see signs for Adventure Park; follow
them and go a ways up the private road. There you'll see the
state's best area for hang gliding. If you aren't inclined to fly yourself, there are several places to watch others. The park also has
the world's first hang-gliding simulator, by which one can experience the feeling without actually being thrown off a mountain.
There are also camping facilities, a camp store, and a water slide
in the park. (615) 825–0444.

Marion County

Farther up Highway 41 just across the county line on your
right, you'll see the sign for the **TVA's Raccoon Mountain
Pumped Storage Facility.** It is the most unusual of all the
Tennessee Valley Authority's operations.

This hydroelectric plant uses more power than it generates.
The safety officers who take you on an amazing hour-long tour
of the plant will usually agree with that arguable fact, but they
will quickly tell you that the plant is very cost-effective.

The visitors center is located at the top of the mountain, about
9 miles from the front entrance, and what a view of the Tennessee River Valley it offers! Also at the top is a 528-acre lake. Deep
inside the mountain is the mammoth power plant, totally pro-
tected from the elements and enemy attack.

At night, during off-peak hours, the extra energy produced at
TVA coal-burning plants is used here to pump water from the
Tennessee River up a 1,100-foot pipeline to fill the reservoir
above. This is cheaper than shutting down and restarting those
plants, and the electricity that would be wasted is now used to
"stockpile" water that will in turn create more power.

During the day, when the demand for electricity is greatest, the
water is released from the reservoir and tumbles down the 35-
foot diameter intake tunnels to turn the four large generators,
thereby producing electricity.

During the free tour, the guide will take you through some of
the 2¼ miles of bored-out tunnels within the mountain. Also,
you'll visit one of the cavernlike rooms, each large enough to

hold twelve tennis courts and with ceilings 80 feet tall. The statistics recited to you will boggle your mind.

There are fewer than two dozen pumped-storage facilities in the United States, and this is the only one that is completely underground. There are several scenic pull-offs on the drive to the top and quite a few picnic areas. At the foot of the mountain, there are fishing areas along the river, all courtesy of the Federal government. Tours are given daily; admission free; (615) 821–0312.

As you pull back out onto Highway 41, take a right and head toward the best catfish dinner or lunch you've ever had. About 6 miles from the TVA, and in a different time zone, you'll find the **Riverside Catfish House** on Highway 41 North on the right next to the river.

The family-run business was established in 1959 and is owned today by Miss Hattie Massengale. Daughters Linda Turner and Donna Caradine work there, as does Turner's daughter. The place seats 125, with many of the tables in front of big windows overlooking the river. "We don't take reservations, so you'll have to get here early if you want a window seat," cautions Turner.

Although they also serve items other than fish, Turner said that 95 percent of the people order the grain-fed catfish dinner, which comes with coleslaw and hush puppies. (In the lobby, there's a picture of a cow and a pig, both begging the patrons to "Please eat Fish.") If you enjoy a cold beer with your catfish, you're out of luck here. "We used to sell it, but the church people complained," Turner said. For dessert, Miss Hattie's famous buttermilk pie is a favorite, as is Turner's coconut cake.

They're open Thursday through Sunday, and although they are on central time, they run by eastern time since most of their customers come from "that side of the line." (615) 821–9214.

If it's genuine homemade yard art that tickles your fancy, Leon Shrum's front yard, on Highway 41 in the northwest corner of the county, just before you get to the county line, should be your next stop. Shrum specializes in "anything people will buy from me."

Among his favorites are pine Dutch windmills, wishing wells, flower pots, lamps, and swings. He sells most of his work to garden centers and open-air markets and does virtually no business out of his home, which doubles as his workshop. If you stop by, however, he'll sell you anything he has in stock at a very low wholesale price. "I don't even get my money back on most of this stuff," he maintains.

There are no signs, but his name is on the mailbox, and there are plenty examples of his work stacked beside his sheds. (615) 592–6534.

Grundy County

One of Shrum's customers is the **Dutch Maid Bakery** in Tracy City. In addition to being the state's oldest family bakery, the store sells local crafts, a sampling of local honey, and other local items.

The bakery, founded by John Baggenstoss in 1902, is now run by John's youngest son, Albert. During the years, all six sons have been involved in the business.

The entire bakery is almost like a museum. Everything but the merchandise is at least sixty years old. Most of the baking is done in a 1930 converted stoker oven.

Possibly best known for his applesauce fruitcake, Albert also bakes salt-rising bread and other "regular bakery items." He still makes most of the local deliveries himself. No formal tours are set, but if Albert is in and has the time, he'd be happy to brush the flour off his apron and walk you through. Open daily; (615) 592–3171.

Stay on Highway 41 and head to Monteagle, where, just across Interstate 24 on Highway 50, you'll find one of the best places for pit barbecue and hickory-smoked meats in the state. Jim Oliver's Smokehouse complex offers a great country store, meeting rooms, a lodge, a motel, and his famous restaurant. In all, he has twenty acres, full of all sorts of things to do. The motel's swimming pool is a sight in itself: it's in the shape of a ham. (615) 924–2268.

Across Highway 50 is the Monteagle Wine Cellars, which offers tours and wine tasting. The establishment of the winery here represents what is hoped to be a revitalization of the area's grape growing and wine making, which was started by a group of Swiss immigrants who settled nearby in 1870. Monteagle is at an elevation of 2,100 feet. Open daily year-round; (615) 924–2120.

Just north of Monteagle off Highway 41 is **Wonder Cave,** the oldest and one of the largest commercial caves in the South. What makes the hour-long tour of this cave so interesting is the fact that lighting has not been installed in the cavern. All lighting is provided by Coleman lanterns. Originally opened in 1900 after being discovered by a few adventuresome college students, the cave is open daily. Admission is charged; (615) 467–3660.

Grundy County is gaining a national reputation as a mountain crafts center, thanks to several artisans whose works are known and in demand from coast to coast. Many of these craftspeople have settled in the center of the county and have established homes and local ties.

In Altamont, woodcarver Ron Van Dyke bought the town's old mill and has rebuilt a couple of its buildings and has plans to restore as much as possible. Greeters Mill pumped water for the town, ground its corn, cut its wood, and was a major operation until 1968.

Today, one of the buildings serves as the home for the Cumberland Craftsman, a shop specializing in Van Dyke's work, as well as that of other local artists. The old wood kiln is now Van Dyke's workshop. Out front, the old steam engine that was used in this operation has been put back together and painted. It's a good landmark for the establishment. Make sure you take a look at his claim to fame, the Hillbilly Chess Set. This hand-carved set features Pa (king), Ma with rolling pin (queen), the boys, with rifles (knights), whiskey barrels (pawns), stills (bishops), and outhouses (castles). (615) 692–3595.

As you head north on Highway 56, you'll see the **Old Wood Village** just before you enter the village of Beersheba Springs. Proprietor William Hassel has moved three old buildings from the area to his property and uses them to live in, work in, and showcase his crafts. After doing the craft-show circuit for about ten years, Hassel decided to quit the rat race and move to Tennessee. While on the juried show route, he earned himself a national reputation for his woodwork.

Among his works, he features various pieces of furniture that combine the art of fine woodworking with mountain twig designs. He also creates and carves out wooden vessels that are shaped like urns and bowls.

Hassel is usually in his shop trying to keep up with the demand of being a one-person business, but he'll always take time to sit down and chat with you about his business or the simple life of Grundy County. (615) 692–3829.

On the other side of Beersheba Springs, Phil and Terri Mayhem live and work in an 1850s log cabin. Phil's work with high-fired, functional porcelain pottery is represented by sixteen galleries in twelve states. Terri creates porcelain jewelry. Phil, a former arts professor, has developed a porcelain that will fuse at a higher temperature, thus making it more durable. Phil and Terri both will show you their work, usually displayed on the front porch of their house during the warmer months. Their business is called Beersheba Porcelain. (615) 692–2280.

Beersheba Springs was a bustling resort area during the last half of the 1800s; and its grand hotel, which was built in 1850, is still standing. Down the road a couple of blocks from the Mayhems, the building is now owned by the United Methodist Church and used as a summer meeting facility. The view from the front of the hotel is nothing less than breathtaking.

When the hotel was active, stagecoaches would stop at the foot of the mountain and sound a horn once for each guest they had aboard for the hotel. By the time they reached the top, the hotel's band was ready to greet them. Dinner and a clean room had also been prepared.

The hotel grounds are the site of an annual arts and crafts show held in late August.

Sequatchie County

High atop Fredonia Mountain, down a series of gravel roads, Greg and Lisa Warren have named their home and acreage **Rivendell Farm.** If you're a J. R. R. Tolkien fan, you'll recognize Rivendell as the name of a valley in *The Lord of the Rings*.

"That's where all the elves lived," said Greg. "Now, llamas live here instead." Greg and Lisa have seven of them and are in the llama-raising business. Their private stock is used for packing and trail rides as well as pets. The Warrens also raise spotted saddle-bred horses, a breed that is rapidly gaining in popularity. It's too hard to give directions to the farm, but Greg said to call him first and he'd tell you how to get there; (615) 949–3868.

Down the mountain in Dunlap, there's a developing historic site that most overlook, mainly because it was the illegal town dump for decades. Through the dedication of volunteers, headed up by Carson Camp, history is being uncovered on the sixty-two-acre **Coke Ovens Historic Site.**

A huge coal industry was present in this area at the turn of the century, and in this Dunlap industrial complex coal was turned into coke for use in the iron and steel foundries in nearby Chattanooga.

When the company went out of business in 1917, there were 268 beehive-shaped coke ovens in operation. Through the years, the ovens were forgotten, covered up, and neglected. During the past few years, Camp and his crew have uncovered a lot of the area's heritage that had almost been forgotten.

The park has been listed on the National Register of Historic Places, and a museum is being built on the original foundation of the old commissary building. Excavation is continuing; meanwhile the park is open, and on some days, you might find Camp or one of his volunteers over in a corner with a shovel in hand. They'll tell you the story. (615) 949–3483.

Warren County

Cumberland Caverns, located about 7 miles southeast of McMinnville on Highway 8, is the second largest cavern system in the United States, behind Kentucky's Mammoth Cave. Unless you happen to be an expert in this sort of thing, most of the tour through the cave reminds you of just about any other cave journey.

One room here, however, is impressive no matter what your interests are. The "Hall of the Magic King" room is 600 feet long, 150 feet wide, and 140 feet high. It is the largest cave room east of the Mississippi River. The room's man-made amenities are built alongside the natural formations. Of these constructed features, the most amazing is the dining room, which will seat 500 for a banquet. High above the tables is a 15-foot, 1,500-pound chandelier from a theater in Brooklyn, New York.

Also in this room, one will see (and hear) a theater pipe organ and a stage equipped for live shows or movies. And all this is more than 300 feet below the hustle and bustle of the real world above! (615) 668–4396.

Cannon County

Priscilla and Harold Woodward own **Harold's Place,** a shop overflowing with quality mountain folk art. Unlike a lot of crafts outlets, this one accepts no consignments. "I buy the work from the artist, add 10 percent to it and resell it. That way we all end up being happy," she claims.

She's eager to share her contacts too. If you buy something and want to talk to the artist about it, she'll give you the artist's phone number. She also encourages each artist to sign and date the work she sells for them.

Husband Harold's contribution to all this may be the best art the shop has to offer. He's a gun engraver and a creator of custom knives. Specializing in Bowie knives, he's one of five Tennessee members in the prestigious Knifemaker's Guild.

You'll be surprised how inexpensive some of the items are when you take away a middleman who wants to make a lot of money. The shop is located at 204 East Main Street in Woodbury; (615) 563–4619.

Up off Highway 96 at the very top of the county is the little community of Auburntown, which claims to have the "Best Little Fish Fry in the South." A tradition that started in 1978 to raise money for the local Lion's Club, the event is the social highlight of the area. Held the first Saturday night of each month in the community center, the dinner is just about the best bargain around, especially if you're hungry.

For $6, you get all the great northern white bass you can eat, along with hush puppies, coleslaw, and iced tea or coffee. There's a huge repeat business from month to month from a five- or six-county radius. It's a great place to catch up on all the gossip.

Dekalb County

The Herndons are having a swine time out on Blue Springs Road, about 8 miles south of Smithville. Jimmy and Fran run **H & H Pig Farm,** a farrow-to-finish pig operation.

Several years ago when they first got the idea, they went to the University of Tennessee for advice. They listened to what the folks told them, and from the building plans to the type of lights to use, they followed all the advice to the inch. Today the operation is one of the most efficient pig facilities in the state.

Tennessee is eighteenth in the United States in hog production, but agriculture as a whole is the state's number-one employment, employing about 25 percent of the state's population. More than 80 percent of the state's land is used, in one form or another, for agriculture.

The Herndons' operation turns out about 2,000 pigs a year from their 100-sow herd. Fran will show you around the farm and explain the whole process, from hand breeding to birthing to nursery time to finishing to shipping. The length of time from birth to market is usually less than six months. If you're calm and nice, she'll let you pet George, her favorite boar. (615) 597–7303.

Putnam County

Cookeville, this county's seat of government, had two early surges of commerce that resulted in two distinctive downtown sections. The town had already established its square and business hub long before the railroads came through. When the rails came to town in 1890, they came through a residential area on the west side of town. That area soon became less residential and more commercial as business shifted from the established area around the courthouse to the new, prospering area around the depot. A large hotel was built, and warehouses and stores soon followed.

By 1910 a new passenger depot had been built, and the area was considered the "Hub of the Upper Cumberland." Passenger service was terminated in 1955, but the locals were able to save the depot, now on the National Register of Historic Places and the site of the **Cookeville Depot Museum.**

Inside is one of the best re-creations of an early depot in the state. Original fixtures, desks, time schedules, and the like have been preserved through the years. There are five rooms of exhibits, plus a caboose out back with more displays. Admission is charged; (615) 528–5550.

Across the street from the museum, high atop an old dairy, you'll see a big, old-fashioned neon sign advertising Cream City Ice Cream. Atop the sign is a giant ice cream sundae whose cherry bounces up and down (in neon) when the sign is turned on. The people who bought the location when the dairy closed chose to not only save but restore the sign to its 1950s beauty. Now, several times each year, the sign is lit, much to the delight of local photographers and nostalgia buffs.

If that makes you hungry, drop by Diana's Bakery at 104 East Spring Street. She has taken a century-old home and converted it into a six-room restaurant, open for breakfast and lunch Monday through Friday. Specialties include her famous chicken pot pies, quiches, crab salad, and various deli sandwiches. To live up to her slogan that her eatery has "The Sweetest Buns in Town," fresh-baked cinnamon and pecan rolls are also offered.

Plan to drop by in midmorning before the local lunch crowd

comes in, grab a bun and a coffee, and head out to the veranda to enjoy the scenery. Open 7:00 A.M. to 4:30 P.M.; (615) 526–6967.

Clay County

In Celina, one will find the oldest **OshKosh B'Gosh** factory in the South. OshKosh, founded in Wisconsin in 1895, is a leading manufacturer of workwear and children's apparel, with a total of sixteen Southeast plants, including ten in Tennessee. The one here was established in 1953 and is really two facilities in one. It is a manufacturing plant and a finishing plant.

A tour of both is quite interesting, but the trip through the finishing plant's laundry is amazing. This is where huge computerized washers stone wash, super bleach, and ice wash denim fabrics to give them the washed-out look so popular today. You've never seen anything like this in your local laundromat!

The plant is located at Westlake and Mitchell streets, just west of the square. The washers are almost always full, since this is the company's only finishing plant in the South. Marian Overstreet is the person who will walk you through. Give her a call in advance if possible; (615) 243–3151.

If you think marbles are just for kids, then you haven't met the gang of marble players here in Celina. For Dumas Walker and his friends, the simple ring marble game is unheard of. What they play in these here parts is called Rolley Hole.

The game is a team sport, played on a 40-foot by 20-foot field called a marbleyard. There are three holes evenly spaced down the middle. The object of the game is for each team of two to get their marbles into each hole in succession, down the court, back and down again, three times.

The top shooters make their own marbles or buy them from fellow townsman Bud Garrett. He'll turn a piece of flint into a top-grade marble on his homemade marble-making machine and sell it for about $25.

No one seems to know why this type of marble playing is so popular around here, but you'll see marbleyards all over town, and just about every night there will be at least one game going on. If you happen to come through town during the day, drop by the Hevi-Duty machine shop, just outside of town. The boys working here are champion shooters and practice out back during breaks.

The Dale Hollow National Fish Hatchery, just north of Celina on Highway 53, produces yearly about 200,000 pounds of 9-inch rainbow trout, which are used to restock public waterways. They also hatch and ship about 500,000 fingerlings each year.

Most of the public waterways in the Southeast are too warm for trout to breed, hence the need for this facility. Trout fishing is allowed and encouraged on most dam and river sites owned by the government, so periodic restocking is necessary.

The hatchery offers self-guided tours, but there are plenty of workers around to answer any questions. A long greenhouse-type of building is where the eggs are hatched, and then the small trout are taken outside to spend the rest of their time here in one of the sixty-four 8-foot by 100-foot concrete raceways.

Feeding times, early morning and late afternoon, are probably the best times to visit. The larger fish are fed food pellets from a truck. A certain amount of food drops down onto a base and then is blown across the water by a current of air. The smaller fish are fed by hand. Open every day year-round; admission free; (615) 243–2443.

Macon County

During the first half of this century, **Red Boiling Springs** was a bustling health and vacation resort known for its medicinal waters. The resort enjoyed its heyday in the years between the world wars, when as many as six large hotels and ten boarding-houses were in business. Today the spa resort feeling hasn't to-tally vanished. The springs are still here, as are three of the hotels, and you can still get a mineral water bath. A major flood in the sixties wiped out much of the old-time charm, but the community has rebuilt and has restored much of that ambience.

The Red Boiling Inn, one of the survivors, has thirty guest rooms available for a flat fee of $25 per day, including three meals. The inn also has the only bath house still in operation. You can "take the cure" here for $15. That includes a bath in black water and an hour treatment. (615) 699–2180.

The town was famous for four types of water: black, red, dou-ble and twist, and free stone. Each is quite different in its mineral analysis and each was considered a "cure" for different ailments. A self-guided–tour brochure of the area is available at the small log visitors center on Market Street.

Over in Lafayette, the county seat, you don't have to have a map to find the biggest loafers in the county. On any fair-weather day, be it in January or June, you'll find a bunch of men of indeterminate age sitting under an old oak tree on the southeast side of the Macon County Public Square. With knife in hand, these whittlers have become part of small-town life around here. The chamber of commerce likes them because of their almost unlimited knowledge of the area. But you don't have to have kin in the area to ask after; just walk right up and start talking with them. But, of course, you'll always walk away wondering whether the directions they gave you will really take you where you want to go or whether these good ole boys have played another trick on a city slicker.

About 5 miles southwest of Lafayette on Old Hartsville Pike, Buck Gammons has found a home for his extensive collection of "junk, antiques, and you name its." A collector for more than thirty years, Buck had been wanting a place to put all his stuff so he could see it all. He found a barn about 2 miles from his house and has been restoring it while stocking it to the beams with his collections.

He started collecting when he lost everything in a house fire. Now he says he can't throw anything away. One of his larger collections is of empty Maxwell House Coffee jars. He hasn't thrown one away since 1955.

He calls his barn the Old Hartsville Pike Roadside Park and Museum. His collection is open to the public, and he'll usually charge $2 per person. "I tell them if they aren't totally happy with what they see, I'll give them the money back when they leave," he contends. So far, he hasn't been asked for a refund.

Although he's officially retired, Buck still "spends too much time working," so a call before you visit would be wise; (615) 655–5460.

Off the Beaten Path in the Heartland

1. Music Row
2. Museum of Tobacco Art and History
3. Greek Parthenon
4. Museum of Beverage Containers and Advertising
5. Twitty City
6. Music Village U.S.A.
7. The Carter House
8. Carnton Mansion
9. Manuel's Cajun Country Store
10. Nissan Motors Manufacturing Corporation
11. George Dickel Distillery
12. Jack Daniel's Distillery
13. Hundred Oaks Castle
14. Falls Mill
15. Carlton's General Store
16. Bell Buckle
17. Wartrace
18. Moon Pencil Company
19. Natural Bridge
20. Village of Hohenwald
21. James Grocery and Cafe
22. Loretta Lynn Ranch
23. World O'Tools
24. Ruskin and Jewel Caves
25. Land Between the Lakes
26. Clarksville–Montgomery County Historical Society
27. Plummer's Old Store and Museum
28. Adams
29. Southeastern Wild Horse and Burro Adoption Center

The Heartland

Davidson County

No matter where you go in the world, mention Nashville to anyone and you'll get a smile of understanding. Ah, country music—that's what most people associate with the state's capital city.

Nashville is one of the areas where the unbeaten path crosses the well-traveled path and merges for a few miles and a dozen or so attractions.

There's no place like Nashville (AKA Music City, Twangtown). Its maternal relationship to country music has created quite a few unique attractions and events. Since the majority of visitors come to see the music-associated attractions, many of the other attractions are ignored to a greater extent than they would be in just about any other city. Five of the region's top ten attractions are country music related.

A hint about getting around: There's a lot of traffic in the downtown and Music Row areas during peak summer periods, and parking spots can be hard to find. Find one and leave the driving to the Nashville Trolley Company. It's 25 cents a ride, or you can buy a book of ten tickets for $2. Unfortunately, the trolleys don't offer service to the outlying areas.

In the northeast quadrant of the city, home to the mammoth Opryland USA, make sure you visit the Nashville Palace, across the street from the entrance to the Opryland Hotel. The Palace, owned by the friendly Johnny Hobbs, is where country superstar Randy Travis was discovered while working as a dishwasher. Live music nightly and a delicious menu that includes "the best catfish in town" are featured. (615) 885–1540.

The world famous **Music Row,** near downtown, offers two atmospheres. First, there's the touristy strip where the stars have their own museums and souvenir shops. Then there's the music-related businesses and studios located along a series of streets with such names as Music Circle and Music Square.

Barbara Mandrell Country anchors the activity along the strip on Demonbreun Street and features the star's memorabilia and a large gift shop. The small restaurant here features the Barbaracue sandwich.

Other smaller museums and establishments of personal salutes in the area include the George Jones Car Museum, Hank Williams, Jr., Museum, and souvenir shops owned by and featuring items of Randy Travis, Conway Twitty, Willie Nelson, and many others.

For the person who wants to stay away from the souvenir shoppers, a stop at the Country Music Hall of Fame is a must. Located at 4 Music Square East, the museum covers the genre from the beginning. Run by a foundation, the facility offers a low-key alternative to the other hubbub along Music Row. A tour of RCA's Studio B complex, the site of early recordings by Elvis and other country icons is also offered by the museum. Admission is charged; (615) 256-1639.

Songwriting is a revered occupation in Nashville. No other city pays attention to its writers the way Music City does, and radio announcers are just as apt to say who wrote a song as who performed it. "Writers' Nights" are held in various locations on a regular basis and are great places to get right down to the basics of country music. Hearing a popular writer singing his or her list of hits that others made into million-sellers is like listening to an oldies jukebox.

Perhaps the best-known cafe in the city, The Bluebird is also one of the best places to attend a writers' night. The food is good, the talent is excellent, and chances are good that you might be sitting next to a country superstar. They hang out here a lot, especially during writers' shows. The Bluebird is located in the Green Hills area of the city, about fifteen minutes from downtown at 4104 Hillsboro Pike; (615) 383-1461.

Just north of downtown, **The Museum of Tobacco Art and History** features a collection of cigar-store figures, a snuff box collection, tobacco-related memorabilia, advertising items, and a noted collection of Meerschaum pipes. A subsidiary of U. S. Tobacco, the museum offers free tours. It's located in that company's manufacturing plant at 800 Harrison Street; (615) 242-9218.

In the heart of downtown lies the Tennessee State Capitol. Finished in 1859, it was designed by William Strickland, who also helped design the U.S. Capitol. The beautiful building is being renovated in stages, and it is undervalued by tourists. Strickland loved the place so much that he requested to be interred in its walls. President James K. Polk is also buried there. Admission free; (615) 741-0830.

Down the street from the Capitol is the Arcade, which is being restored to its finest. It was built in 1903 as a two-tiered shopping

The Parthenon, Nashville

mall, an identical copy of one in Milan, Italy. Today, it is occupied by specialty shops, including the mandatory roasted-nut store, whose aroma pervades the entire complex.

Several decades before the city was known for its music, it had a reputation as a regional center of culture and education. Numerous colleges advanced the learning of the classics, and it wasn't long before the city was known as the Athens of the South. In 1896, it was only natural for planners of the state's centennial celebration to elaborate on this classic theme.

An exact replica of the **Greek Parthenon**, with a tolerance of less than 1/16th of an inch, was built for the huge exposition, held in what is now known as Centennial Park, just a few miles out West End Avenue from downtown. The newly restored Parthenon now houses art exhibits and serves as a backdrop for various cultural events in the park. A 42-foot replica of *Athena Parthenos* is in the process of being sculpted. Admission is charged; (615) 259–6358.

For the best fried chicken and country ham dinners in Middle Tennessee, follow West End Avenue (it turns into Highway 100 farther out) to the Loveless Motel and Cafe. It's about 15 miles from downtown. Owner Donna McCabe has herself a neat piece of roadside Americana here, including a colorful neon sign. The food is served family style, with fresh biscuits and homemade preserves. While you're waiting for a table, be sure to read the clippings on the walls. This place has been visited by some very important people through the years, including Captain Kangaroo. It's located in a little house, so reservations are almost a must. (615) 646–9700.

If you're a beer can collector, the **Museum of Beverage Containers and Advertising** might very well be heaven for you. It's located about 16 miles north of Nashville in the small community of Goodlettsville. Their collection of 25,000 soda and beer cans is claimed to be the largest in the world. In addition, the museum has more than 5,000 antique soda bottles on display and a great display of advertising pieces used by various bottlers during the years. Admission is charged; (615) 859–5236.

Sumner County

Across the county line from Goodlettsville in Hendersonville, country music again reigns as king. **Twitty City,** the home, office, and museum of entertainer Conway Twitty, offers a glimpse into the life-style of this superstar. The nine-acre complex has live entertainment during the summer months and a gift shop and a concessions area. From Thanksgiving through the first week of January, more than 350,000 lights and numerous holiday events keep the place active. Locals call the winter event "Twismas at Twitty City." Admission charged to parts of complex; (615) 822–6650.

Music Village U.S.A. is located adjacent to Twitty City and offers four different "showcases" of country music legends. There are the Marty Robbins Memorial Showcase, Ferlin Husky's Wings of a Dove Museum, Bill Monroe's Bluegrass Hall of Fame, and the Willie Nelson Showcase. During the summer months, there are live "Super Star Concerts" in the village's amphitheater. Admission charged; (615) 882–1800.

Williamson County

The country stars and the top bankers and businesspeople of the state might make their millions in Nashville, but when it comes to investing in their life-styles and families, many come south to this county. It consistently has the state's highest per capita income and the lowest unemployment rate.

Maps that show where many of the stars live are available at most bookstores. Dolly Parton, Gary Morris, The Judds, Tom T. Hall, Minnie Pearl, and Waylon Jennings are among the inhabitants of the area. If you want to see them, you probably have a better chance hanging out at the local Krogers store than in front of their houses.

Franklin, the county seat, is 17 miles south of Nashville and is associated with old, restored homes and businesses, antique shopping, and the Civil War. The entire downtown section is on the National Register of Historic Places.

The **Carter House,** south of downtown on Columbia Avenue, was caught in the middle of the fight aptly known as the Battle of Franklin on November 30, 1864. Bullet holes are still evident in the main structure and various outbuildings. Ask the guide to tell you the story of how the owners hid their horses in the attic to keep the soldiers from stealing them.

The property is one of the eleven historic sites in the state owned and operated by the Association for the Preservation of Tennessee Antiquities. Open daily; admission charged; (615) 791–1861.

Across the street is a group of twelve small specialty shops collectively known as Carter's Court. The major eatery is The Bunganut Pig, an English-style pub. Great food, drinks, and atmosphere. Children are more than welcome. (615) 794–4777.

About 5 miles away, the **Carnton Mansion** also played an important role in the Battle of Franklin. On the rear lines of the Confederate forces, the elegant estate witnessed a steady stream of dying and wounded during the battle. At one time, the bodies of five slain Confederate generals were laid out on the back porch. Within view of that historic porch rests the only privately owned Confederate cemetery in the United States. Open daily; admission charged to house; cemetery free; (615) 794–0903.

A few blocks east of the town square, where the Confederate monument (circa 1899) rests, is the Hiram Masonic Lodge. When the three-story building was built in 1823, it was said to be the tallest structure in Tennessee. It was constructed to house the first Masonic Lodge in the state, chartered in 1803, and later, in 1827, the first Protestant Episcopal Church in Tennessee was founded here.

The Catholic church next to the lodge was built in 1871 from bricks fired on the site. Today, the church owns land on both sides of the lodge and has virtually built around it.

Rutherford County

One mile from downtown Murfreesboro is an obelisk marking the geographic center of the state. "The Dimple of the Universe," as it is called locally, is on Old Lascassas Pike. Turn left off Greenland Drive opposite the football fields at Middle Tennessee State University.

Farther out Highway 96, just past Lascassas, lies the small unincorporated village of Milton. With a population of about 200, the place has two businesses, the mandatory post office and **Manuel's Cajun Country Store.** The latter is the place to be.

Among the shoelaces, dog food, and video rentals are red-checked oilcloth-covered tables that come alive four nights a week with the best Cajun food in the state. Abe and Dottie Manuel head up the family operation, while the rest of the family cooks and serves the fried alligator (in season), shrimp, crayfish, and other ethnic specialites.

On Friday nights, the Cajun band, headed by Joe Manuel, fills the streets of Milton with music as it plays from the front porch and people dance on Main Street. Even the Manuel relatives still living in Lake Charles, Louisiana, are involved in the business. They trap the gators the restaurant serves.

Usually a reservation isn't needed, except for the crayfish boil on Wednesdays. Hours are from noon to around 11:00 P.M.; (615) 273–2312.

One of the most interesting factory tours in the state is located north of Murfreesboro, just off Highway 41. The **Nissan Motors Manufacturing Corporation** Truck/Auto Plant offers tours on Tuesdays and Thursdays. During the forty-five–minute trek through the modern plant you'll see men and women working arm and arm with more than 230 robots to produce the 500 vehicles that the plant turns out each day.

You'll see some workers dipping parts into paint while others slam doors. The complex covers about 800 acres and employs a great many of the locals. To be safe, it's best to call ahead to see if they are planning on giving tours the day you want to be there. Admission is free, but of course they don't give samples. (615) 459–1444.

Coffee County

If you happen to be in Manchester the fourth week of June, make sure you have a pair of clean pajamas with you. That's the weekend when the "World's Largest Pajama Party" is held on Courthouse Square. Lots of dancing, bed races, and contests last all night long. (615) 728–7635.

On Highway 55, just before you reach Tullahoma, be on the lookout for the Coca Cola Bottling Company plant. Next to it is the Company Store, a retail outlet open to the public. You'll be amazed at how many things are made with the Coke logo on them. It's a virtual plethora of Coke red and white merchandise, from clothes to antique reproductions to glasses. Open Monday through Saturday, 10:00 A.M.–6:00 P.M.; (615) 454–1030.

It wasn't soft drinks that George Dickel of **George Dickel Distillery** had in mind when he and his wife arrived in Tullahoma in the 1860s. He was searching for the right water to make whiskey. He found the townsfolks sipping a limestone water from nearby Cascade Spring; he investigated, liked what he tasted, bought some land, and in the early 1870s opened his distillery.

The facility closed in 1911 when the state went dry but was reopened by Schenley Distillers in 1958 when the county voted to go wet again. Today, the whiskey is still made the old-fashioned way, and all through the free tour, people are reminded that this is not bourbon but Tennessee sour mash whiskey. The difference is in the charcoal-mellowing process.

Miss Annie runs the George Dickel General Store, located across the wooden bridge, which spans Cascade Creek. Ask her how you can be recognized for your good taste, and she'll hand you an application blank for the George Dickel Tennessee Whiskey Water Conservation Society. Head north on Route 41A from Highway 55 for about 5 miles and then turn right on Marbury Road and follow the signs. Tours are weekdays only. Admission free; (615) 857–3124.

Moore County

Deep in this dry county, you'll find another, possibly more famous, distillery known for its Tennessee sour mash whiskey. **Jack Daniel's Distillery** put Lynchburg, a community of 360 residents, on the map.

Mister Jack (as he was locally known) founded his business in 1866 and received the first federal license ever issued for a distillery. It still holds that number-one distinction.

If you want to take a tour, make sure you wear comfortable shoes: there's a lot of walking and hill climbing. This is true history and Americana at its finest. They'll even let you taste the sour mash by dipping your fingers into the vat during the tour, but since this is a dry county, no samples are permitted.

One of the highlights of the tour is the visit to Daniel's office, left virtually the way it was when he died. Make sure you ask the guide to show you where Mister Jack lost his temper one day, eventually causing him to experience a slow, painful death.

Free lemonade and sugar cookies are available at the visitors center. Nothing is for sale here, but the employees will direct you into the village of Lynchburg to the bevy of shops there. If you're looking for a wide range of Jack Daniel's items as well as crafts and old-time items, the best place to visit is the Lynchburg Hardware and General Store on the town square.

Across the square, Miss Mary Bobo's Boarding House still dishes out the best meal in town. Miss Mary started her business in a pre–Civil War building in 1908 and served many a meal to Mister Jack and visiting VIPs. Because the seating capacity is only sixty-five, reservations are almost a must for the family-style meals. The local wags call it the Bobo Hilton. Lunch is the only meal served, and it's on the table promptly at 1:00 P.M. Adults pay $8.75 and have a choice of two meats, six vegetables, bread, beverage, and dessert. Kids eat for $4.00. (615) 759–7394.

Franklin County

The old Franklin County jail in Winchester had one of the nicest views that any prisoner could ever hope for. Located along the banks of the Boiling Fork Creek, the structure, built in 1897, served as the county's penal institution for seventy-five years. When the new jail was built, the property was turned over to the county's historical society, which then turned it into the Old Jail Museum. In addition to the museum, the cell area and the maximum security cell block are retained as they were. (615) 967–0524.

Heading west on Route 64, you'll see one of the few large castles still left in America. **Hundred Oaks Castle** was built by

Arthur Handley Marks, son of the state's twenty-first governor. Marks traveled extensively through Europe and decided on his return to the family farm that he would build a castle around the existing structure.

What you see here is not the finished castle he had in mind. He died in 1892 of typhoid fever at the age of 28. If there were any plans for the building, they were haphazard at best. Turrets, towers, arched windows, and rounded columns are randomly placed along the 100-foot-long roofline, seemingly placed there on a whim.

"He wasn't an engineer; he was a country gentleman who wanted a castle. He never finished it, but what we have here is an architectural wonder," claims Deborah Rains, the director for the facility. A restaurant is on the ground floor now, and tours are given. Open every day; admission is charged; (615) 967–0100.

When you leave the castle, continue west on Route 64 and you'll head into Davy Crockett country. You'll be going by a roadside marker designating "Kentuck," the homestead that he left in 1812 to go off to the Creek War. He and his first wife, Polly, and their children settled near here when he came back from the war. She died in 1815 and is buried in an old cemetery overlooking nearby Bean's Creek.

If you want any further information on Davy Crockett's ties with this part of Tennessee, stop by **Falls Mill** near Belvidere and talk with owner Janie Lovett. In addition to her duties at the mill she owns with her husband, John, she's active in the local historical association and seems to know everyone in the area.

The Lovetts bought the mill in 1984 and have been busy restoring since. Built in 1873, the mill has operated as a cotton-spinning and wool-carding factory, a cotton gin, a woodworking shop, and a grist and flour mill through the years. Since 1970, it has also served as a sort of museum. But it wasn't until the Lovetts bought it that it started realizing its true potential.

Make sure you take a walk down to the river behind the mill to get a good view of the falls and the 32-foot overshot waterwheel, which is believed to be the largest still in operation in the country. Also, if the miller is working, ask him to show you how to tie the traditional miller's knot.

Grain is still ground and is available at the mill store, along with other local items. A weaving exhibit upstairs in the mill is being created, as is a reconstruction of an 1836 log stagecoach inn that will eventually serve as a bed and breakfast.

Currently, an 1895 log cabin has been move here and reassembled and serves as a bed and breakfast for up to four persons. Rates for the cabin range from $48 to $53 per night for four people. The mill and picnic grounds are open daily. Admission is charged; (615) 469–7161.

Bedford County

Shelbyville, the county seat, is also the center of Tennessee's horse country. It plays host each year to the Tennessee Walking Horse Celebration, an event during which the World Grand Champion is named.

This special breed of horse, developed during 150 years of selective breeding, is promoted today as the "world's greatest show and pleasure horse." The horse has an unusual rhythmic gliding motion in which each hoof strikes the ground separately in an odd one-two-three-four beat.

The breed emerged from the plantations around here during the later part of the nineteenth century but today can be found across the country. The area around Shelbyville is still known for its farms, and most of the owners are happy to show off their facility. Many have signs out welcoming you, but you might want to call the Breeders Association in advance. There may be a special event or training session at one of the farms that you'd find interesting. (615) 359–1574.

While you're in Shelbyville, stop by Pope's Restaurant on the square for the best deep-fried chicken livers in the state. Further north on Highway 41A, business at **Carlton's General Store** in Rover is good. "Sure is—we sell something just about every day," claims owner Earl Carlton. "But the world is trying to crowd us out."

Carlton, a character in his own right, has a small room next to his store where the locals come to solve all the world's problems. They start arriving about 5:30 A.M. and spend most of the day whittling and talking. "They whittle all the time and never make anything," complains Carlton, who is the seventh generation to live within a 2-mile area of the store.

Nobody seems to know exactly how Rover got its name, but the most accepted story is that a bunch of bickering regulars at a local drinking establishment decided to name their community. After hours of arguing over a name, one of them piped out, "Why don't we just call it Rover—we all fight like dogs anyway." So be it.

Along Route 269 in the northern corner of the county lies the

Stop sign at Walking Horse Hotel, Wartrace

quaint little village of **Bell Buckle.** The business district is chock-full of antique and craft stores and has one of the finest quilt stores in the state.

The village is also the home of Webb School, a prepartory school that has produced ten Rhodes Scholars and the governors of three states. The Junior Room, the original wood-shingled one-room schoolhouse built in 1870, has been preserved as it was then, complete with pot-bellied stove and teaching paraphernalia. It's open for visitors daily and is free. The school hosts a well-respected art and craft festival at the end of each October. (615) 389–6045.

Wartrace, down Route 269 a piece from Bell Buckle, also has a few antique shops, but its claim to fame is the world-famous Walking Horse Hotel and restaurant. The first world champion

Tennessee walking horse, Strolling Jim, lived in the stables behind the hotel and is buried out under an oak tree. People are allowed to visit the stables and the well-marked grave.

The hotel was built in 1917, a time when a great deal of its guests came by train. The tracks are still located within a stone's throw of the charming rocking chair–bedecked front porch of the establishment.

The Walking Horse Center is housed in the hotel, and the owner organizes presentations to acquaint guests with the special breed. The hotel has twenty-five guest rooms, and to enter one is truly a step back in time. There are few, if any, modern frills in this hotel. It is being restored, room by room, without altering any of the hotel's old-time atmosphere. Room rates range from $28 to $38, with suites going for $52. (615) 389–6407.

Marshall County

For a reason no one can really explain, this area of the state is a haven for pencil manufacturing. Lewisburg's **Moon Pencil Company,** the nation's fourth-largest pencil company, is the only one that offers tours of its plant. Founded in 1961, the company specializes in non-yellow, specialized pencils that more often than not are sold to advertising-specialty companies, which imprint various messages and logos on them and resell them.

On the tour, you'll get a close-up look at how the pencil, the one item you've probably used since childhood, is made. It's a four-step process, ending in the tipping (inserting erasers) and packing room.

Also in Lewisburg is Faber Casteel, the nation's second-largest pencil producer. The largest, Empire Pencil, has its operation in nearby Shelbyville. Moon's plant manager, Doris Landtroop, is the official tour guide. (615) 359–1501.

Wayne County

Davy Crockett launched his political career during a speech he made from the "pulpit rock" area of the **Natural Bridge,** about 10 miles east of Waynesboro off Highway 64 (Davy Crockett Highway). This bridge is believed to be the only double-span natural bridge in the world. The area also served as hiding grounds for bandits who relied on the nearby Natchez Trace to bring them a continuous supply of weary travelers. Open daily; admission charged; (615) 722–9218.

Mike McDonald makes a living giving buffalo rides. Situated north of Waynesboro, 4 miles off Highway 13, McDonald's operation is nestled along the banks of the Buffalo River.

He provides weeklong trail rides, daylong treks, or half-day adventures. A campground, which serves as the base for the operation, is surrounded by 30,000 unfenced, wild acres. Rides are given only during special periods throughout the year, so call for schedules first. (615) 888–2453.

Lewis County

The Natchez Trace is truly a road trip back in time. The 450-mile road has been a major highway between Nashville and Natchez, Mississippi, since the late 1700s. It is preserved today as a scenic two-lane parkway with few intersections, no commercial activities of any kind, and numerous pull-offs at historic stands (resting areas usually placed one day's travel from the other). The parkway, completed to Tennessee Highway 50 near Shady Grove, will eventually extend to Nashville; its entrance will sit across from the Loveless Motel and Cafe on Route 100.

One of the early travelers on the trace was Meriwether Lewis, the famed leader of the Lewis and Clark expedition. In 1809, he met a violent and mysterious death at Grinder's Stand. His grave is marked by a broken column, symbolic of his broken career. The monument is located near the intersection with Tennessee Highway 20.

The trace is overlooked by those in a hurry because the 50 MPH speed limit is monitored quite closely. Also, make sure you have a lot of gas before you set out. For a map and other details, call (615) 796–2921.

The **Village of Hohenwald** is a junker's paradise. The downtown streets are lined with junk and secondhand clothing shops, and people come from miles away to do their bargain hunting. Used clothing is brought in from the Midwest and Northeast in bales and dumped on the floors of the shops. The bales are broken open each Wednesday, Saturday, and Sunday, the days to be there for the best selection. If you're knowledgeable about brands and clothing quality, some real big bargains await you here. There are tales about people finding money and even diamond rings in the old clothes.

Hickman County

In the small community of Brushy, about halfway between Hohenwald and Centerville on Highway 48, you'll find a prime example of preserved southern culture. Discount stores, supermarkets, and large auto services, which have collectively closed down a lot of mom and pop operations, have not been able to put Betty and Bobby James out of business. The two own the **James Grocery and Cafe.** Outside you'll be able to pump yourself a tank of gas, and inside you'll be able to buy a can of Spam or a tube of toothpaste or have your chainsaw sharpened. But if you look beyond all those crackers, you'll see the real ritz to this operation . . . the cafe.

This cooking and feeding part of the James venture was an afterthought. You won't even see "and Cafe" on the sign outside. You'll just have to be surprised, or be looking for it.

Betty does the cooking and baking in this "meat and three" eatery. Specializing in southern plate lunches, she offers a meat (different each day), three vegetables, and homemade biscuits or bread for $2.75. Chicken and dumplings are a favorite of her regulars, as are her cobbler and fruit pies.

Special orders? Sure, why not. Call ahead and tell her what you want, and she'll do her darndest to have it ready for you when you show up. That's the advantage of having a restaurant in a grocery store. Open from 7:00 A.M. to 5:00 P.M., six days a week; (615) 729–3181.

Humphreys County

The coal miner's daughter not only lives in Hurricane Mills, she owns it. When country music's most-awarded female vocalist, Loretta Lynn, and her husband, Mooney, were house shopping back in 1967, she was searching for a big old "haunted looking" place. When she saw this century-old mansion, she knew this was her dream. She wanted it immediately, not knowing the entire town and old mill came with it. The **Loretta Lynn Ranch,**

79

on Route 13 in Hurricane Mills, is her home as well as her museum and special place to welcome fans.

In 1975 a campground was developed, and since then numerous other attractions have been added to the ranch, including Loretta's personal museum, a replica of the coal mine her father worked in, a replica of her "Butcher Holler House," and a gift shop.

Tours of the first floor of her antebellum plantation mansion are given daily. Make sure you ask the guide about the haunted aspects of the building. There is no charge to enter the ranch, but there is for the tours, museum, and other activities, including miniature golf and canoeing. There are dances every Saturday night during the summer, and Loretta schedules a few concerts during that time also. When she's home, she enjoys walking around meeting the people and signing autographs. (615) 296–7700.

A few miles north on Route 13, Hunter Pilkinton lives out his fantasy in his **World O'Tools.** "Everybody needs a world of something," said the lifelong collector. "Mine happens to be tools." Hunter's world contains more than 20,000 tools of all sorts and a large library of books and pamphlets about those tools. The museum is the result of a hobby that got out of control. Several barns and sheds on his property contain his treasures.

The retired, personable Hunter has a story for each one of the items, and he'll tell you each one. It's best if you call first. "I may be out hunting for more tools and miss you." (615) 296–3218.

Along the Tennessee River at Highway 70 is the Johnsonville Tennessee Valley Authority (TVA) facility. Built in 1950, it was the TVA's first major coal-fired power plant. Tours are given when "someone shows up who wants one." The length of tour and how long you might have to wait for one to start can vary depending on the work load of the staff at that particular time. It's most likely they'll find time for you Monday through Friday in midmorning or midafternoon.

One of the things to look for during the tour is the coal-unloading facilities. If you're lucky enough to be there on the day the coal is being unloaded from a barge, you'll see a huge crane in operation that is capable of unloading coal at a net rate of 700 tons an hour. The coal then goes by conveyer to the crusher building, which is a sight in itself. After you leave here, you'll have a real appreciation for electricity and the work that goes into producing it. (615) 535–2561.

Dickson County

Although many people think of Dickson County as their own utopia, most don't realize that their county was inhabited by a group searching for the perfect life in the late 1800s. Before the attempt failed in 1899, the thriving colony centered in what is now **Ruskin and Jewel Caves.**

That attempt, the last major effort to create a true utopian society in Tennessee, was led by Julius Wayland. Enthralled with the socialistic writings of Englishman John Ruskin, Wayland printed a newspaper espousing those social theories. The circulation grew, and he promised his readers that the profits would be used to buy land for a socialist colony. His intent was to create a practical, functioning model of social reform. As is true of most utopian attempts, Wayland's had inherent problems, which would eventually be its demise. (See the Rugby utopian attempt in the Morgan County section of chapter 2.)

Wayland raised enough money to buy acreage in Tennessee City and built the colony, named after his mentor, Ruskin. By August 1894, Wayland and a few followers had started creating the colony. But within two years, he resigned as its leader and the colony moved to an area 5 miles away.

By early 1897, there were about seventy-five buildings built along the Yellow Creek, and about 250 residents from thirty-two states and six foreign countries were living here. More strife took its toll, and by late 1899, Ruskin had run its course, and an auction was held.

Following the collapse of Ruskin, the buildings and land became a school named Ruskin-Cave College. After it closed down, it became a resort with the big three-story structure, built by the Ruskinites, being used as a resort hotel. Then the land and buildings went through a series of owners.

Today, the property is owned by James Gill. Ruskin Cave is a Christian counseling center for predelinquent teenage boys, and Jewel Cave reopened in 1989 as a commercial cave. The large hotel structure is still standing and has been placed on the National Register of Historic Places with plans to restore it. The grounds at Ruskin have a large swimming pool, tennis courts, and a whole array of activities that are open to the public.

James Gill is proud of his holdings and has great plans for them. He'll be glad to show you around the Ruskin Cave area and send you over to see Bill Anchors, who runs Jewel Cave for him. Anchors is a true historian and can give you all sorts of additional information about the early Ruskin socialist community. He's also the cave tour guide.

There's a small fee to use the facilities at Ruskin and for the tour of Jewel, but admission is free if you just want to go into the Ruskin area and look around. It would be wise to call Gill before showing up. Ruskin: (615) 264–1401. Jewel: (615) 763–2651.

Stewart County

The 170,000-acre peninsula between Kentucky Lake and Lake Barkley is owned and operated by the Tennessee Valley Authority and is aptly called the **Land Between the Lakes,** or LBL, as locals refer to it. About a third of it lies in Tennessee and the rest in Kentucky.

The area is an awesome display of nature. The Trace, the main north-south road, is 60 miles long, with southern entry just west of Dover, off Route 79. There's plenty to do here, and according to the rangers, most of the area is underutilized.

In addition to all the hiking trails and water activities, there are more than 100 miles of paved roads for biking. The Homeplace is a nineteenth-century living-history museum with sixteen restored structures that were moved from other LBL locations and rebuilt. Costumed personnel work the farm, and most will take time from their chores to talk history with you.

Homeplace employees eat here, with all food prepared over the open fires and in the kitchens of the restored buildings. While walking through the kitchens, talk with the cooks. They have some great stories to tell about their past cooking experiences.

Across the trace from the Homeplace, the largest federally owned herd of buffalo east of the Mississippi River roams the range. Here, the range consists of two 100-acre fields that hold up to fifty head of buffalo. Each animal needs about four acres to live and eat.

Although the American buffalo is associated with the western plains, herds ranged the Tennessee hills as well. In fact, many of the roads and highways in the state today follow old buffalo trails. If you want to see the herd, make sure you get there early in the morning. They have a tendency to disappear into the woods as the heat of the day increases.

There is a fee for many of the attractions, but to view the

buffalo or hike the trails there is no charge. There are several special events during the year that the LBL newsletter covers in detail. Call for a free copy; (502) 924–5602.

Dover's Town and Country Restaurant, specializing in southern cooking, is a favorite among the locals for a good meal. You can order from the menu or partake of their buffet from 11:00 A.M. to closing each day except Sunday. A special seafood buffet is offered on Friday and Saturday nights. Reservations are suggested for Saturday, especially during the summer. Open seven days a week from 5:00 A.M. to 10:00 P.M.; (615) 232–6930.

Montgomery County

Although it has to share honors with Kentucky, Montgomery County is the home of the famed 101st Airborne Division–Air Assault of the U.S. Army. The Fort Campbell Military Reservation covers more than 100,000 acres on the state line and is the county's largest employer.

The base is open, which means visitors are welcome as long as they pick up a pass at Gate 4 on Highway 41A. Located near the gate is the visitors center and the Don F. Pratt Memorial Museum. Named after Brigadier General Don Pratt, who was killed while leading the 101st Airborne's legendary glider assault into Normandy, the museum traces the history of the division from World War I through the present. Exhibits also depict the history of Fort Campbell and the land it occupies.

Probably the most interesting exhibit in the place is the replica of the fragile-looking glider that the members of the 101st Division used in France during the D-Day invasion of 1944. More than 14,000 of the canvas-covered cargo gliders were built during the war, with such unlikely businesses as the Steinway Piano and Heinz Pickle companies contributing to the effort.

Across the street from the large indoor portion of the museum is a lot with a large collection of tanks, artillery field pieces, and airplanes. Open every day; admission free; (502) 798–3215.

Clarksville is the state's fifth-largest city, with a population of about 60,000, but it probably has the largest selection of architectural marvels of any one city in the state. "Anyone interested in architecture will have a field day in Clarksville," maintains Carolyn Miles, curator of the **Clarksville–Montgomery County Historical Society.**

Any tour through the city should start at the historical society's headquarters at the corner of Commerce and Second streets. Originally constructed as a U.S. Post Office and Customs House in 1898, its eclectic architecture consists of Italinate ornamentation, Far East–influenced slate roof, Romanesque arches, and Gothic copper eagles perched at each of the four corners.

Exhibits inside include one on the local tobacco industry and a salute to the local firefighters. This is one of the finest local museums in the state. Area tour maps can be picked up here. Open Tuesday through Sunday; admission is charged; (615) 645–2507.

There are two self-guided tours of the city and county—a 2-mile (twenty-five site) walking tour of the downtown architectural area and a 14-mile (fifty site) driving tour. One of the highlights of the walking tour is the Madison Street Methodist Church. Built in 1829 by a Jewish architect, the Star of David appears in the construction in at least two locations. Presumably they weren't discovered until the architect got paid.

Mildred and Henry Plummer have had a great time running their little store for the past thirty-some years. **Plummer's Old Store and Museum,** located a few miles out of Clarksville on Highway 76 East, reflects that three-decade relationship. The seventy-five-year-old clapboard building, with berry bushes partially hiding the signs on the sides, does one of two things to a passing motorist. It either beckons him in or scares him away. And the latter would be quite a shame.

The Plummers are hospitable people who have lived next to their store for all but two years of its existence. Between the two structures, vegetable plants, fruit trees, and purple martin houses can be found. When they leave for church, they leave produce on the porch and change for $10, just in case someone needs something while they're not there.

At lunch, they spread out sandwich makings on a table in the store and let people create their own meals. Henry enjoys a good joke as well as anyone, and Mildred says people come just to hear his stories and to be had by his practical jokes. One corner of the store is set aside for "fun and silly" items. A large flat rock lies on the counter with the painted words, "Please turn me over." When you do, the painted message reads, "Thank you, that's much better."

Possibly the biggest draw is the museum. Henry estimates he has more than 1,000 items in the back of the store, separated from the rest of the establishment by chicken-wire. A sign on the door explains what's back there. "Pre-electric and plastic, Granny's things, and Granpa's tools."

You'll never see a more eclectic collection in your life—from cherry pitters to slave shackles and chains to a chicken-head cutter. Henry is more than eager to walk you through and explain each item. Most of the stuff was given to him by people who knew he would take care of it for them. The Plummers are what true southern hospitality is all about. There's a small admission fee for the museum. (615) 358–9679.

Montgomery County's answer to California's Napa Valley can be found at the Beachaven Vineyards & Winery, a few miles off I-24's Exit 4. Co-owner Ed Cooke thinks his winery can offer as good a tasting tour as his counterparts in California. "We offer the same thing, but we add southern hospitality." he said.

Beachaven's "taste till you like it" concept is a great plus for those needing a little education before buying a wine. Ed or one of the employees will be glad to give you a taste of all their varieties. Tours are given year-round for those who would like to see how the fruit of the vine becomes so divine. And these wines are real divine! Wine judges across the country think so too. Look at all those ribbons lining the walls awarded to the various products of Ed and his family. Their champagne is of "world renown," having been written up in the major wine books.

The most exciting (and aromatic) time to visit is in the fall while the crushing is taking place, but there is always something going on. During the summer, special concerts are presented in the vineyard's picnic area. They can't sell by the glass, but they would be glad to sell you a chilled bottle to enjoy with your cheese during a concert. (615) 645–8867.

Robertson County

There have been ghosts and there have been legends, but the Bell Witch of **Adams** is probably the most documented story of the supernatural in all of American history. This witch is unique because of the large number of people who have had direct experience with it.

John Bell was a well-respected and influential member of the Adams community. He and his family lived on a thousand-acre plantation along the Red River. The trouble started in 1817 when bumping and scratching sounds were first noticed, but the Bells passed them off as being caused by the wind. The big problems started in 1818, when continuous gnawing sounds were heard on each member of the family's bedposts each night. When someone would get up to investigate, it would stop. The sound would go from room to room until everyone was awake. Then it would stop until the candles were blown out and everyone went back to bed, when it would start all over again.

Things grew from there. People came to town to witness the occurrences and weren't disappointed. General Andrew Jackson came up to Adams from his Nashville home to investigate the matter but turned around when the wheels on his carriage mysteriously locked.

This has gone on through the decades. A few years ago, several reporters came to Adams with plans to stay in the Bell cave, where many of the experiences have occurred. They lasted a few hours before fleeing.

Today, the cave is sporadically open to the public for tours. All the Bell buildings are gone now, except for a small, log slave building. It has been moved to the grounds of the old elementary schoolhouse and is open for viewing. You can't miss the graves of the Bell family at the Bellwood cemetery. There's a magnificent tower marking the graves and a stone fence keeping the Bell Witch out.

The best place to start your tour of Adams is at the old school that is now known as the Bell Witch Village Antique Mall, run by Nina Seeley. She was a neighbor of Elvis Presley in Memphis but convinced her husband to move to Adams after reading about the witch. She's quite the promoter of the Bell Witch legend.

She's also the founder of the Bell Witch Opry. For the past sixteen years, the opry has been held each Saturday night at 7:30. It's a country music show featuring Nina, as well as some up-and-comers who just might show up on the Grand Ole Opry in the next few years. The show is held upstairs in the old schoolhouse. Admission is $5 per couple, one of the best entertainment values in this neck of the woods. (615) 696–2762.

The Tennessee-Kentucky Threshermen's Association holds its annual wheat threshing and steam engine show at the school during the last part of July.

If you've ever wondered where those wild horses and burros that are rounded up from the western wilds go, you need not wonder anymore. Many of them come to Cross Plains and are adopted out of the **Southeastern Wild Horse and Burro Adoption Center.** On any given day, the pens are full of animals from Nevada, Arizona, New Mexico, and California waiting for new homes.

The adoption program is a partial solution to the problems of overpopulation among wild horse and burro herds that roam public rangelands in ten western states. When this facility opened in 1979, it was the East's first waystation for these animals. The center is run by Randall and Paula Carr on their 200-acre farm and is funded by the federal government.

Each year during the first weekend in July the center holds the Tennessee Wild Horse & Burro Days celebration and invites those who have adopted to bring back the animals and compete in the Middle Tennessee Mustang Association Horse Show. The adoption center is off Highway 25, just outside the village of Cross Plains. There's no charge unless you take a horse or burro home with you. In that case, it'll cost you up to $125. Open year-round, Friday through Sunday; (615) 654-2180.

Off the Beaten Path on the Western Plains

1. Tennessee River Folklife Center
2. Culpepper's Store
3. Tennessee's First Driver's License
4. Kingdom of Skullbonia
5. Doodle Soup Capital
6. Guy's Grocery and Cafe
7. White Squirrels
8. Obion County Museum
9. Dixie Gun Works
10. Reelfoot Lake
11. Carl Perkins Square
12. Alex Haley House Museum
13. Tennessee Woods Art Gallery
14. Casey Jones Home and Railroad Museum
15. World's Third Largest Pecan Tree
16. Shiloh National Military Park and Cemetery
17. Buford Pusser Home and Museum
18. Little Courthouse
19. Flying Feathers Quail Farm
20. LaGrange
21. Bozo's Restaurant
22. Beale Street
23. Mud Island
24. Peabody Hotel

The Western Plains

Benton County

Nathan Bedford Forrest, the notorious hard-riding Confederate cavalry officer known for his unexpected and often off-beat tactics, pulled off one of the Civil War's most interesting victories along the Tennessee River here in the fall of 1864. It was probably the first time in military history that a calvary force attacked and defeated a naval force. High atop Pilot Knob, the highest point in this part of the state, Forrest secretly assembled his troops. He had his eye on the Union army's massive supply depot, directly across the river.

At the time, the depot had more than thirty vessels, most fully loaded, waiting to head out to Union forces. Stacks of supplies lined the wharf. Forrest attacked and caught the Yanks off guard. Within minutes, all thirty vessels and the various warehouse buildings were on fire, and within two hours everything was destroyed. By nightfall, Forrest's troops had vanished into the dense woods.

The land surrounding Pilot Knob is now known as the Nathan Bedford Forrest State Historic Area. Atop the hill is a monument to Forrest. Also at the top is the **Tennessee River Folklife Center,** "designed to explore the relationship between the river and the people who use it."

Most of the exhibits incorporate segments of oral histories taken from the locals who "lived the life." Separate accounts recall the early industries, and the music, religion, and community events of the area.

The most colorful audio presentation highlights the days when folks would gather around the river to welcome the big showboats to their landing. The biggest exhibit is "Old Betsy," an entire workboat from the early musseling industry along the river. The most visual representation of early river life is from the Brownie camera of Maggie Sayre. She lived on a houseboat for more than fifty years and photographed everyday life around her.

Most rural areas throughout the South have their own version of the liar's bench and the spit and whittle club. The view from the porch or from under the tree may be different from town to town, but the plot is the same. A story is told, then retold, then exaggerated to the point where it becomes a modern-day myth. A typical riverfront liar's bench has been reconstructed here at the center, with a breathtaking view of the Tennessee River far below. Walk up, push a button, and sit down and relax. The series of taped stories (from original spit and whittlers) will keep you in stitches.

The center is open daily. Admission free; (901) 584–6356. The historical park area offers camping, hiking trails and picnic areas. Both areas are located at the end of Highway 191, about 10 miles out of Camden.

John Latendresse has developed his own techniques for developing freshwater pearls in mollusks taken from the nearby Tennessee River. He is regarded as the first person in America to culture pearls. From an idea in a lab in the early 1960s, his pearl venture has grown to include four companies and more than 120 employees. Much of the technique is still considered "secret" by Latendresse. The mussel is implanted with a nucleus, which then "grows" into a cultured gem, known as the Tennessee Pearl. The process takes from one to three years, depending on the type of mollusk used and the type of pearl being cultured.

Many of the pearls are used by American Pearl Creations, also owned by Latendresse, to make jewelry for its 3,000-plus clients. Because of the secret nature of the pearl culturing, tours of that end of the business are somewhat limited at particular times, but there's plenty to see in the jewelry-making end of things. (901) 584–8290.

Tennessee ranks twelfth in the nation in sorghum production, and Benton County is one of the largest producers in the state. Madison and Donice Furr run the Tennessee Sorghum Company, one of the largest operations in the county.

Sorghum is mainly used as a sweetener and is rich in vitamins. It's used in gingerbread and is poured over hot biscuits and butter. "It's very good and very healthy for you," claims Donice. "We sell a lot of it to health food stores."

The Furrs grow about thirty acres of sorghum cane and produce their own syrup. They also buy from other Benton County sorghum producers and market the product under the Tennessee Sorghum Company moniker.

The most aromatic time to visit the Furrs' operation is in the fall when the sorghum cane is being stripped of its juices and cooked down to the right consistency. The cooking is done down at the Furrs' farm, and the marketing and packaging takes place at their warehouse in Camden.

Donice welcomes visitors to the farm and promises to let them "stick a finger" in the cooking sorghum for a once-in-a-lifetime taste treat. The farm is located off Highway 192, about 5 miles north of Holladay. Call her and see if anything is going on the day you want to go out, and she'll give you specific directions. (901) 584–3322.

Henry County

There's no place better than an organized wildlife refuge to observe that area's wildlife population, and the Tennessee Wildlife Refuge is no exception. Hiking paths, paved roads, and observation points are plentiful in this 80-mile-long area along the Tennessee River. The area is an important resting and feeding place for migrating waterfowl each winter.

Beginning about mid-October, up to 100,000 Canada geese and 250,000 ducks start their annual fall trek to the refuge where they will spend the winter. The major attraction here for the animals is the farming program, which provides them with a great deal of food all winter long.

In addition to the waterfowl, the refuge is home for more than 200 species of birds, a fact that brings in serious bird watchers from all over the country. Maps, brochures, and specific wildlife information is available. Open daily, year-round; (901) 642–2091.

In nearby Paris, the "World's Largest Fish Fry" is held at the end of each April. Since the early 1950s, the city has hosted the event at the fairgrounds and has achieved a (well-deserved) reputation for the quality of its catfish dinners and the traditional Tennessee way of preparing them.

Each year more than 8,500 pounds of fish are cooked in black kettle pots containing more than 250 gallons of vegetable oil. The four-day event also includes a rodeo, a carnival, a three-hour parade, and a fishing rodeo.

The fish fry, the hunting, the fishing, and the proximity to Nashville were but a few of the reasons that country singing superstar Hank Williams, Jr., chose this area for his Tennessee home and business offices. A few miles out of Paris on Highway 79 East, Williams has his Kaw-Liga Korners, a combination retail store and office complex. He lives farther out of town. (901) 642–6900.

For a good bologna or ham and cheese sandwich, or for a

bucket of minnows, crickets, worms, or chicken livers, stop by **Culpepper's Store.** Owners Trenton and Rita Ward can usually be found there, as can Nicky Poo, their poodle. "We call ourselves a country place inside the city limits," Rita said. The small store specializes in bait and fishing supplies, as well as food and drink for the fishermen. Rita, who was born in Germany, is a favorite among the returning servicemen at nearby Fort Campbell. "As soon as they get back from Germany, they come in and want to show me how much German they learned while they were over there. It's also fun for me to hear about their impressions of my country."

Look for the American flags flying just inside the city limits on Route 69A. Even if you don't need any bait, stop by, Rita and Trenton will tell you about the area and some of the people who live around here. Open every day.

Down Highway 79 is the small city of Henry, which might be the only city in the state with its executive offices housed in a log cabin. A few blocks down the street, you'll find Annie's Cafe, specializing in "country cooking." It's also housed in a log cabin.

Carroll County

Gordon Browning's first driver's license is on display at the Gordon Browning Museum, in the old post office building in downtown McKenzie. What makes that license so special is that it is **Tennessee's First Driver's License.**

Browning got it because he happened to be governor of the state in 1938, when licenses were first required. In all, Browning served three terms as governor. He was also a U.S. congressman and a county judge, and he served in both world wars, and by the looks of the quantity of the memorabilia on display, he never threw anything away. A flag that he brought back from World War I is on display, as are various other patriotic mementos.

The museum is a great small-town collection dedicated to the life of the county's favorite son. It gives a good perspective on the values that he and the curator of the museum deemed important.

Mary Ruth Debault is the curator for the county historical society and probably knows more about this man than any living soul. The museum is open every day except Monday and Tuesday. Admission is charged; (901) 352–5741.

Signpost, Skullbone

Gibson County

When bare-knuckled pugilism was popular and legal in America during the first half of the nineteenth century, one area of this county was well known for its unique version of prize fighting sans gloves.

Skullbone and the surrounding **"Kingdom of Skullbonia"** hosted a type of fighting that became known as skullboning. All bare-knuckled punches had to be delivered to the head. Hits below the collar were not permitted and considered fouls.

To "play," fighters would stand opposite each other and take turns trading blows. Each round lasted until one would fall to the ground. The match lasted until one was satisfied that he had had enough.

After bare-knuckled fighting became illegal in America and communities went "underground" for the excitement, matches in Skullbone continued to be held in the open. When adoption of standard rules for prize fighting occurred in 1866, non-gloved activities died out just about everywhere except Skullbone, where it continued well into the twentieth century.

Today, just about all that remains of Skullbone is the general store, built in 1848. It has been owned since 1964 by Landon and Ruby Hampton and is known locally as Hampton's General Store, widely as the Skullbone Store.

The busy little store serves what is left of the "kingdom." Yellowed newspaper clippings of the area's heyday hang on the wall. Outside, the building is quite a landmark. With a map of the Kingdom of Skullbonia painted on one side and various soft drink signs and paintings on the front, a stranger can't drive by without stopping to investigate.

Across the street, a stacked row of directional road and mileage signs point the way to worldly centers such as Singapore, 9,981 miles, Anchorage, 3,320 miles and Shades Bridge, 1 mile.

In addition to the regular fares of a country store, the Hamptons sell souvenir t-shirts. Skullbone isn't on most maps, but the Hamptons are trying to get Tennessee's governor to put it on the official state map. It's located on Highway 105, about 3 miles from Bradford. Open every day; (901) 742–3179.

It's amazing that just 3 miles away from the skullbone capital of the world one can find the **Doodle Soup Capital** of that same world. In fact, Doodle Soup is so popular in these parts that a festival is held in its honor each September.

What is Doodle Soup? It's a cold-weather dish, not good during summer because of its spicy nature. It's actually more of a sauce or gravy than it is a real soup. One of the most popular methods of eating it is by pouring it over a plateful of cracker crumbs or home-made biscuits, and letting it soak in for a while before eating.

Here is one of the "official" recipes. Be forewarned: There has been a battle going on for years as to which of the myriad of recipes floating around should be considered official.

Take a large broiler chicken. Melt butter and rub chicken all over. Put in broiler pan, split side down; salt to taste. Put in oven at 375 degrees; let cook until brown and tender. Take chicken out of the drippings that were cooked out in the pan. Add eleven cups of water, one cup vinegar, plenty of hot peppers, three table-spoons of cornstarch so it won't be just like water and will stay on biscuits good. Let cook until it gets as hot as you want. Taste it along.

Although it's a local tradition, most locals haven't eaten it, say-ing it sounds too "greasy." One restaurant, Jer-E-Lane, is rumored to have it on the menu occasionally.

About 3$1/2$ miles west of nearby Trenton on Highway 104 is **Guy's Grocery and Cafe,** a place that many people feel serves the best catfish and chicken in western Tennessee. Guy's is an-other country store that has turned to food service.

Hollis Guy bought the store back in 1951 and sold groceries and pumped gas for years. One night back in the early 1970s he fired up a big black kettle and cooked a mess of catfish for his fishing friends. That dinner went over so well that the cafe idea was born.

Guy does most of his business from an attached room that used to be an apartment, although there are some tables in the store itself. He's closed Mondays, and his big meals are served in the evenings, but he does offer sandwiches for lunch just about every day. A nighttime, all-you-can-eat buffet is served Thursdays, Fridays, and Saturdays and features chicken, catfish, french fries, hush puppies, white beans, coleslaw, sweet onions, pickled beets, and assorted "chef's specials." The price is $7 per person and includes all you can eat and drink, dessert, and tax.

On Sundays, Guy serves up a noontime buffet that includes most of the same food but goes for $5. He's humble about the raves his food receives, and says he only has one secret. "If you cook fish, you gotta change your cooking oil frequently."

His success has him thinking about expanding his nighttime hours. No reservations are taken, but get there early on Friday and Saturday nights. (901) 855–2920.

In Trenton at the municipal building you'll find the world's largest collection of eighteenth- and nineteenth-century night-light teapots (*veilleuses-théières*). A New York doctor, originally from Trenton, was going to give his multimillion-dollar collection of 500 pieces to the Metropolitan Museum of Art in New York City, but his brother convinced him to give them to his hometown instead.

Originally displayed in the trophy cases at the local high school, the unique collection found a permanent home when a new city building was built. The teapots now line the walls of the city's chambers. If you get there during regular business hours, you're welcome to walk around and study this one-of-a-kind collection. If you happen to get there late, a sign on the front door directs you to the firehouse where a friendly firefighter will hand over the key to city hall on the promise that you'll lock up and return the key before you leave town. Admission free; (901) 855–2013.

Up Highway 45W from Trenton is Rutherford, where a former home of Davy Crockett is open to the public. David (as residents prefer him to be called) moved to the area in 1823. His original cabin, built 5 miles east of town along the Obion River, was dismantled and stored with the intent of rebuilding it at a later date near where his mother is buried. But before it could be rebuilt, most of the logs were used in fires by campers.

Some of the logs were saved and are now a part of the reproduction of that original cabin. On display are tools, furniture, and utensils from the period, as are letters that Crockett wrote home during his years in congress. A rocking chair that Davy made is also on display.

The cabin is open from the end of May to the third weekend in October each year. It's located on the city's grammar school property, on Highway 45W. Admission is charged; (901) 665–7166.

Farther up Highway 45W you'll find an amazing colony of **White Squirrels,** one of only a few such colonies in the world. As you enter Kenton, a town of about 1,500 residents, you'll be greeted by a big sign proclaiming, "Kenton. Home of the White Squirrels." Although the exact number is hard to pinpoint, as most white squirrels look alike, the city's official stance is that about 200 of the critters live here. The squirrels are fed by just about everybody, and there's a $50 fine if you kill one.

A wildlife biologist explains that the animals are actually "albino gray squirrels who have survived for so long because the people have taken such good care of them." They have in-bred for so long that the normally recessive albino trait has become predominant.

Exactly how the first such squirrels came to the area about 120 years ago is the subject of a great many speculations. The most common theory is that during the early 1870s a band of Gypsies spent the night on a local farm. The next morning, in appreciation of the farmer's kindness, the leader of the Gypsies presented two white squirrels to the farmer. Thus it began.

The best time to see the flock (bevy? herd?) of white squirrels is in the morning and evening when they are most apt to be scurrying from tree to tree. Stop by the city hall, which also informally serves as a white squirrel visitors information bureau.

Obion County

The **Obion County Museum** in Union City is the only regional history museum in this part of the state. All the other museums are specialized, so this is the place to go to get a good overview of what northwest Tennessee is all about.

County historian Rebel C. Forrester is the perfect guide as he walks you through the displays and explains little tidbits of history that only a county historian would know. A collection of "documentary" photos from 1915–23 gives a good visual feeling to the other exhibits. Among the items on permanent display are a Model-T Ford, Indian artifacts, and a horse-drawn hearse. Open on a rotating basis every couple of years is a 1920s kitchen that shows the before-and-after effect of electricity on a Tennessee home.

Adjacent to the museum is a two-room log cabin with exhibits. The museum is open Saturday and Sunday afternoons and is located at 1004 Edwards Street, directly behind the high school. Admission free; (901) 885–6774.

About a block from the museum at the end of Edwards Street is the first monument erected in honor of the unknown Confederate soldier. It was dedicated on October 21, 1869. Some of the twenty-nine buried died in training at Camp Brown, here in Union City.

Gun collectors worldwide probably already know about this city's **Dixie Gun Works,** while noncollectors across town may have never heard of it. Founded by Turner Kirkland in the early 1950s, the business is now considered the world's largest supplier of antique guns and parts. The firm sells about 80,000 guns a year, including antique reproductions.

At any given time, a walk through the Dixie Gun Works' showroom is like walking through an antique firearms museum, except that you can buy most of the guns you see here. Usually, more than 1,500 guns are on display. Kirkland's other passion, antique automobiles, is also in evidence. Adjacent to the gun showroom is an auto musuem with more than thirty cars, including a 1908 Maxwell.

A small log cabin gunshop is a part of this attraction. Originally built in this area around 1850, the shop contains two rifling machines and more than 1,000 gun-making tools. The complex is located on the Highway 51S Union City By-Pass. Admission charged for museum; (901) 885–0561.

North of Union City on the Kentucky border lies the early railroad center known as Fulton. Today, the city of Fulton is in Kentucky, while South Fulton is in Tennessee, although there is barely a line of demarcation.

The thing that made this railroad center different from most is that the city had the largest one-floor ice plant in America. The early railroad refrigerated cars needed ice, and this place had plenty to offer. One of the first refrigerated items that was transported and thus required stops at numerous ice houses was the banana.

It wasn't long before this small town was the redistribution center for 70 percent of all bananas brought into America. For more than six decades, the community held that distinction. Now, to revitalize that heritage, the communities hold the International Banana Festival each September.

The four-day event includes banana-eating contests, parades, and the making of the world's largest banana pudding. The 2,000-pound creation is made by a local dairy and is the highlight of the parade as it cruises by in a special see-through plastic vat. At the end of the parade, the pudding is scooped into 10,000 individual containers and given away free to the crowds.

There's not much left of the old Fultons now; the railroads don't even come through town anymore, and the ice house burned down several years ago. But the library keeps the heritage alive year-round with available information and exhibits on this once-thriving tropical industry. (502) 472–2975.

The Jack Flippen family, all three generations of them, are actively involved in the family's Flippens Hillbilly Barn business, just outside Hornbeak, about 12 miles from Union City. Originally established as an orchard, various parts of their business have grown from circumstances.

The Hillbilly Barn still sells apples and peaches but is into much more. Several years ago, the Flippens started selling apple cider and individual fried fruit pies at the encouragement of a local festival promoter. They have been frying pies and making cider since.

Mrs. Flippen started frying hamburgers when an orchard worker forgot to bring his lunch one day and asked her to cook something for him. Now the snack bar is open seven days a week, Monday through Saturdays from 7:00 A.M. to 6:00 P.M. and Sundays from 1:00 to 6:00 P.M. A large patio built over the lake allows outdoor seating, and an outdoor entertainment stage offers various types of live music. The homemade jams and jellies are quite popular, but through it all, the apple and peach fried pies remain the major reason for much of the return business. More than twenty-seven varieties of apples and peaches are also available.

To find the establishment, head west out of Union City on Highway 22. Go 8 miles and turn off the highway onto Shawtown Road, and go 8 miles to the barn. (901) 538–2933.

Lake County

About ten minutes west of the Hillbilly Barn is **Reelfoot Lake,** the result of a true quirk of nature. The worst earthquake ever measured in American history took place in this area in 1812. On February 7, the quake hit, and the lands of northwest Tennessee near the Mississippi River dropped as much as 20 feet.

For fifteen minutes the river's water flowed backward to fill this major void, which had been a swampy forestland. Now, the area is a 13,000-acre shallow lake, 6 to 8 feet in depth, with the remains of the forest just under the surface, which makes boating quite an adventure. The water is a dark green color, with visibility never more than a few inches. The area surrounding the lake is now a state park, and a journey through here is truly a trek into unspoiled nature. The combination of shaggy cypress trees, some of them centuries old, and water lilies is most unusual for this state.

Because of its uniqueness, the lake's boaters were forced to create a special type of boat for easy navigation. Known as a "stump jumper," the boat is pointed at both ends, has a flat bottom, and is powered by a one-cylinder lawnmower engine that is capable of operating in 6 inches of water.

Reelfoot Lake is also the winter home to more than 100 American bald eagles. The birds, with wingspans of 6 to 8 feet, come here from their northern summer homes to spend the winter in a warmer, ice-free environment. The park provides numerous eagle programs, including bus tours of the area during winter.

The park's museum offers the chance to experience an earthquake, first hand. The 1812 quake has been reproduced, to a lesser degree, and allows guests to feel and hear what took place during those fifteen minutes. You can also sit in a stump jumper, learn about its creators, the Calhoun family, see Indian artifacts, and read first-hand accounts of the creation of the lake. The museum is also the loading site for the lake's sight-seeing cruises.

The park has camping sites, a camp store, rental cabins, and hiking trails. Guided hiking trips are offered during the year. A resort inn and restaurant, both owned by the state, are built out over the lake among the cypress trees. The entrance to the park is located off Highway 21.

An annual calendar is produced listing the best times, month by month, to see the various wildlife around the lake. A copy can be obtained by calling the ranger's office; (901) 253–7756. A three-day arts and crafts festival is held each October at the park.

Of the world's talented songwriters, Carl Perkins is among the few who can actually say they helped launch an entire era of music. In Memphis during 1955 a young entertainer named Elvis Presley recorded the Perkins-composed "Blue Suede Shoes" and created a whole new sound in the process.

Perkins was born just 2 miles from Reelfoot Lake, in Tiptonville. His museum is now located at **Carl Perkins Square** and is filled with memorabilia including gold records, autographed photos of the era's greatest stars, and the original copy of the song that started it all, written on two brown paper bags.

In addition to the music history in the museum, the complex has a record store, an arcade with nickel pinball, an ice cream shop with an old-fashioned soda fountain, and a souvenir shop. Open daily except Monday; (901) 253–8346.

Lauderdale County

Henning, the boyhood home of author Alex Haley, is a picturesque town of Victorian homes and turn-of-the-century storefronts. The town probably would have progressed quietly like many small towns had it not been for native son Haley.

His 1976 Pulitzer-prize–winning novel, *Roots*, and the subsequent TV miniseries, based on the family stories his grandmother and aunt told him, brought international fame to Henning, where Haley's family home is now the **Alex Haley House Museum.**

Those stories inspired Haley to research his family members, who were brought to America as slaves, and the book came as a result. He recalls sitting on the front porch of his boyhood home and listening for hours to the stories.

Haley's museum by description is a "tribute to Kunta Kinte's worldwide family." Built in 1918 by a Kunta Kinte descendant, the house has been restored and not only serves as a tribute to Haley but also as a good example of rural small-town life in west Tennessee. It is also the first Afro-American state historic site and the only writer's home open to the public in Tennessee.

The museum is located at 200 South Church Street at Haley Avenue and is open Tuesday through Sunday. Admission charged; (901) 738–2240.

In a bright red caboose in downtown Henning, the area's historical society has its records and artifacts on display at the heritage museum. Open by chance or appointment; (901) 738–5055.

Crockett County

Crockett County was established in 1871 and named in honor of the famed Tennessee frontiersman Davy Crockett. The county seat of the 14,000 residents of the county is Alamo, where the *Crockett Times* newspaper is published.

Crockett had already been killed when the county was formed, so when it came to finding a name for the new county, locals thought naming an entire county after the man would be an appropriate tribute. Cageville was renamed Alamo and became the county's center.

Crockett never lived in the county and there is no record that he ever visited here, but the people are proud of their living monument to one of the state's best-known sons.

Madison County

While many of his fellow craftspeople headed out to areas where "the tourists are," Larry Sellers settled on an area in the northern portion of the county, along Highway 45E. "I've been real surprised—I get a lot more tourists and out-of-state people in here than I ever dreamed I would."

Sellers is a wood carver and chain-saw artist and president of the **Tennessee Woods Art Gallery,** an outlet for his and his friends' creations. A "born-again Baptist," Sellers decided to go into business for himself in 1984 with little more than faith in his "God-given" talent that he believed he had to use or lose. He is now one of the most sought-after artists in this part of the state.

As you pull up to the front of the gallery, a large, hollowed-out cypress log about 15 feet tall greets you. He makes these logs into unique treehouses. As you walk into the shop, a life-size Nativity scene attracts your attention. The twelve-piece set sells for about $9,000, and Sellers says he sells two or three a year. A large mountain man, which he says is slowly replacing the cigar-store Indian as the most popular wood carving, also greets you as you enter.

Sellers says the most requested item in his chain-saw line of art is the hillbilly figure, used almost exclusively as yard art. "It seems everybody wants a hillbilly in his front yard this year," he said. If you have a dead tree in your yard, he'll come out and carve a hillbilly for you out of its trunk for about $1,500. (901) 783–3265.

Farther south, in Jackson, construction on the city's first modern waterworks in the 1880s led to a discovery of one of the area's most prolific underground mineral water rivers. That powerful mineral spring, known as the Electro Chalybeate Well, still bubbles forth its clear waters. Through the years, thousands of people have come to its source searching for a cure for their internal ailments.

Shortly after the spring was discoverd, a public park was developed around the spring and a lake was created. The area became quite an attraction for residents, and social life in the Jackson area soon revolved around the park. The park and the lake are both gone today, but a gazebo has been built over the remaining well, where people can still come to take the cure. The well is next to the city's restored art deco water plant, about three blocks from the town square.

"Come all you rounders if you want to hear a story about a brave engineer." That's the beginning of the tale of Casey Jones, an engineer who became a legend after being killed in a much-publicized train crash. The **Casey Jones Home and Railroad Museum** tells the story of that fateful night. Casey was at the throttle of "Old 382" when it approached a stalled train on the same track near Vaughn, Mississippi, on April 30, 1900. The fireman jumped and yelled to Casey to do the same, but he stayed on and valiantly tried to stop the train. He didn't, but he slowed it down enough so that he was the only casualty of the wreck. The engineer immediately became a folk hero, and his story has been recounted for more than a half-century in story and song.

Casey was living in Jackson at the time of his death. His home has since been moved and now serves as the centerpiece of the museum, located in Jackson's Casey Jones Village on the Highway 45 By-Pass, just off Interstate 40. In addition to the museum, the village contains specialty shops, and the Brooks Shaw and Son Old Country Store, a country restaurant complete with an 1880s-style soda fountain and large gift shop. Shops are free; admission is charged to the museum, which is open daily, year-round; (901) 668–1222.

Henderson County

Covering 43,000 acres, The Natchez Trace State Resort Park is Tennessee's largest state-run facility. It is also the home of the **"World's Third Largest Pecan Tree."** The tree is 106 feet tall, has a spread of 136 feet, and was planted in 1815. Legend says that one of General Andrew Jackson's men returning home from the Battle of New Orleans gave a pecan to a man called Sukey Morris, who then planted it because he didn't want to eat it.

The size of the tree is quite impressive, but what is more amazing is that the tree has been chronicled, by photos, almost since its "birth." Those photos are on display at the park's visitors center. The tree still gives a few pecans, but as one ranger said as she looked up at the tree, "It's hardly worth the effort to try and eat one. They aren't that good."

The massive park, with its lakes, trails, and heavily forested areas is a success story for one of President Roosevelt's New Deal programs. When the U.S. Department of Agriculture acquired the land in the early 1930s, the area was some of the most heavily abused and eroded land in the state. The area's occupants were relocated, and a "Land-Use Area" project was set up to demonstrate how wasteland could again be made productive through proper conservation practices.

Picturesque Pin Oak Lodge and restaurant, situated in a heavily wooded area of the park next to a lake, offers some of the best food and lodging in this part of the state. Cabins, a swimming beach, family camping, off-road vehicle trails, fishing, boating, and miles of hiking are other attractions at the park. Open year-round; (901) 968–3742.

Decatur County

Each April coon hunters gather at the county fairgrounds just south of Parsons on Route 69 to take part in an event that is billed as the "World's Largest Coon Hunt." Depending on the year and the weather, about 600 hunters from thirty to thirty-five states come here to hunt for the state's "official" animal, the racoon.

This is basically a competition for dogs, so no guns are allowed and no coons are hurt. The hunter with the dog who does the best "tracking and treeing" goes away as the winner. Since coons are nocturnal, most of the action on this weekend takes place at night. A country band plays until 3:00 A.M., and the local Jaycees keep their concession stands open around the clock for the entire weekend.

The event is considered to be the biggest independent fund raiser for St. Judes Children's Research Hospital in Memphis. More than $100,000 is raised and donated each year.

Farther south on Route 69 is the county seat town of Decaturville. In downtown, Ed's Restaurant serves ribs one night each weekend. "That's pretty much the highlight around here when the coonhunt isn't going on," said the owner of the town's gas station.

Hardin County

The **Shiloh National Military Park and Cemetery,** 12 miles south of Savannah on Route 22, is a grim reminder of how bloody the Civil War really was.

On April 6 and 7, 1862, the North and South fought the first major battle in the western theater of the war here, just a few miles north of the Mississippi state line. More than 23,000 soldiers, about one-fourth of the total forces that fought, were killed. The deaths in this one battle exceeded the total American casualties from the nation's three preceding wars, the Revolution, the War of 1812, and the Mexican War.

Known as Bloody Shiloh, the battle went down in the history books as one of the most gruesome. The park was established in 1894 and includes the battlefield and environs. A 9-mile self-guided auto tour is available that highlights the battle and explains the various monuments that have been erected. The visitors center has a library and a museum, complete with relics and maps and a movie explaining the battle. Open daily, year-round; admission free; (901) 689–5275.

McNairy County

The signs along Highway 64 outside Adamsville proclaim the community to be the "Biggest Little Town in Tennessee." A lot of that obvious pride may come from the fact that the town was home to one of America's most celebrated lawmen, Buford Pusser.

Pusser, who died in an auto accident in 1974, is immortalized today in the **Buford Pusser Home and Museum,** located at 342 Pusser Street. He was sheriff of this county from 1964 to 1970 and had the reputation of a no-nonsense, hard-nosed lawman. The exploits of this 6-foot, 6-inch tall, 250-pound "legend" were the basis of the three *Walking Tall* movies.

Today, in the quiet residential area that he called home, his brick ranch house is overflowing with artifacts of his life. Following his death, his mother moved into the house and allowed nothing to be removed. Opened officially in 1988 as a museum, the facility is owned by the state and is leased and run by the city. Everything from his credit cards to his toothbrush to the roll of $50 bills he had in his pocket when he was killed are on display. An advertisement from a mattress company rests on his bed. "Big Buford Bedding, designed to honor a man who walked tall in Tennessee."

The years he spent as sheriff were hard ones on this "soft-spoken country gentleman." He was shot eight times, knifed seven times, and gunned down in an ambush that killed his wife. Many residents feel the flaming auto crash that took his life was no accident.

According to the museum's hostess, Jimmie Powers, Pusser was constantly on guard and often remarked that he was "on borrowed time." His home is a reflection of that attitude. He had a special entrance built on the lower level, where his underground bedroom and living quarters were. He slept with his head against the earthen wall to help protect himself against the continuous threats.

In addition to his personal belongings, numerous scrapbooks of newspaper clippings, a videotape of television interviews, and a copy of his 1956 high school yearbook are on display. Dwana, his daughter, can often be found at the house talking with visitors. Admission is charged; (901) 632–4080.

Up Highway 224 near Leapwood, the Coon Creek Science Center reveals that this whole area was under a sea about 85 million years ago. The center, opened in late 1989, is owned and operated by the Memphis Museum System, although it is more than 150 miles from that city.

When emptied, the warm, shallow ocean left behind an abundance of unusual and significant geological treasures. The marine shells found here in the bottomlands are not actually fossils but the real things, since they have not undergone the process of mineralization and have not turned to stone. The clay of the area has preserved the shells in their original form.

Known as the Coon Creek fossil formation, the entire area attracts geologists from all over the world. The center has been established to preserve the area and to provide an educational facility for the study of the earth sciences. Plans call for the creation of various exhibits and programs. If you'd like to see a part of Tennessee that few others have, call and arrange a time to visit. (901) 454–5600.

The hog is king at Pappy Johns whole hog barbecue, located on Highway 45 South, a few miles outside Selmer. Here, you gotta be hungry for pork, because that's the only meat served. Open daily except Sunday, pork ribs are cooked up three nights a week, Wednesday, Friday, and Saturday, while the rest of the hog is available all the other times. A good deal of the business here is take-out, but if you enjoy eating near the hickory pits where the cooking is done, there are·tables inside. (901) 645–4353.

Less than a mile down the road from Pappy Johns is the sprawling Kings Antiques. Located in more buildings and sheds than you can count from the road, Kings' sign says that it has more than 15,000 items and that it sells used cars and appliances as well as antiques and collectibles. It also offers small-engine repair. Open daily except Sunday and Monday.

Along Highway 57 just east of Ramer city limits, you'll find a nice piece of folk art in the Deming family's front yard. A tall bicycle sculpture, made out of old wagon wheels. and various other pieces of "junk," the item is a true piece of roadside Americana.

Across the street from the bicycle is the Comic Strip Cafe, where "laughter is always on the menu." Good food is what they serve with a smile here. Especially good are the catfish dinners. Open daily.

Hardeman County

The county's first courthouse, now known as the **Little Courthouse,** was built in 1824, making it one of the oldest original courthouses in western Tennessee. Located at 116 East Market Street in Bolivar, the restored structure now houses the county museum.

The original part of the existing building was a two-story log structure that served as the courthouse. In 1827 the building was purchased and moved to its current site, where additions were made to the log structure. It was converted into a family residence in 1849 and more additions were made, turning it into a large Federal-style home.

The building itself is worth the stop, but some of the items inside highlighting this county are fascinating in themselves. Open by appointment or by chance; admission charged; (901) 658–6554.

Another historic structure in Bolivar is The Pillars, former home of John Houston Bills, one of the original settlers of West Tennessee. Built prior to 1826, the building saw the likes of James K. Polk, Davy Crockett, General U. S. Grant, and Sam Houston. It served as military headquarters during the Civil War. It is currently being restored but is open on occasion. Admission charged; (901) 658–6554.

The Magnolia Manor is this area's premier bed and breakfast. The 1849 structure has been completely restored to its early splendor with wooden floors throughout. Owners James and Elaine Cox currently run the three-guest-room inn. Rates to stay at the antebellum inn range from $45 to $50, including a choice of meals. Located at 418 North Main Street; (901) 656–6700.

The Anderson Fruit Farm is considered the state's largest orchard. Covering 250 acres near Cloverport, the farm has more than 25,000 apple, peach, and pear trees in an area better known for its cotton production than fruit.

In addition, corn, peas, sweet potatoes, tomatoes, squash, okra, green beans, melons, and blackberries are all raised here and sold in season. More than 10,000 gallons of apple cider are made and sold each year.

Visitors can pick their own peaches and apples during the proper seasons, with rides to the orchards provided on a hay wagon. The Andersons welcome guests to their orchards, on Highway 138 in Toone, but their fruit and produce are also available at their roadside market in nearby Whiteville. (901) 658–5524.

Quail hunting is a big sport in the southern part of the county. Sporting clubs specializing in quail hunting are dotted across the bottom part of the state. Not relying on Mother Nature, owners of these clubs buy quail and release a certain number in a field for their paying customers.

One of the bird suppliers is the **Flying Feathers Quail Farm,** just south of Highway 57 near Saulsbury. More than one covey of quail can be found here at Joe Jordan's bird farm. He specializes in American bob whites and admits that it can be quite noisy around the farm at times.

"It's my job to raise a bird that is as close to a wild bird as possible," claims Jordan as he carefully walks among the young chicks. Once the chicks are old enough, he puts them in a fly pen where he encourages them to learn to fly. The 50-foot by 120-foot fly pen is crucial to their "wild bird" education.

The birds are sold to the preserves when they are about 14–16 weeks old. Jordan will take you on a tour of this facility and might give you a couple of eggs to take home and fix for breakfast. He says they are very good for you. Call for directions; (901) 764–2950.

About 7 miles west on Highway 57 is the small community of Grand Junction, home of the National Field Trial Championships. Held at the 18,600-acre Ames Plantation since 1896, the annual February event is often called the "Super Bowl of Bird Dogs."

Competition lasts eight to ten days, with the winning dog earning the title of World Champion Bird Dog. Hunting mostly for quail, the dogs and handlers are followed by a large gallery of spectators on horseback. As quail raiser Joe Jordan says about the mounted spectators: "There must be 4,000 or 5,000 of them out there at a time. They never see a dog, but they sure have a good time."

The plantation, although synonymous with the quest for canine excellence, plays an integral part in the University of Tennessee's livestock and agriculture program. The facility is one of the eleven branch experiment stations in the university's system. Built in 1847, the plantation is open to the public on the fourth Thursday afternoon of each month from March through October. Admission free; (901) 764–2167.

While Ames Plantation is the official headquarters, Dunn's Supply Company, in downtown Grand Junction, is the gathering place for local as well as international bird dog aficionados. The store carries just about anything one would need for bird hunting and other outdoors activities. In the back room, the owners have created a hall of fame for the past champions of the National Field Trials. Admission free; (901) 764–2193.

Fayette County

Heading toward Memphis on Highway 57, you'll find **La-Grange,** a quaint little village that has been able to avoid the commercialization that the others have fallen to along this busy highway corridor. In addition to a couple of antique shops, the streets are lined with a plethora of well-kept little white cottages with green shutters and trim. Settled in 1819 on the site of an Indian trading post, it was named for General La Fayette's ancestral home in France. Translated to mean "beautiful village," it was occupied by Union forces from 1862 to 1865. It was an antebellum center of wealth, education, and culture, having had two colleges, four academies, two newspapers, and 3,000 residents in 1862.

Tipton County

In Mason, just across the county line on Highway 70, is **Bozo's Restaurant.** Look for one of those tiled cafe buildings that dotted America's landscape a while back, and you'll find Bozo's.

Founded in 1923 by Bozo Williams, the restaurant has stayed in the family and is now owned by the founder's great-grandson, Jeff Thompson. Famous for its pork shoulder barbecue sandwiches and plates, Bozo's has a full menu that has not changed since shortly after World War II.

When he took over ownership in 1988, Thompson was told by "just about everybody" not to change a thing. One thing he did do, however, was to bottle and sell the establishment's popular sauces. Food comes with no sauce, allowing the diner to choose between the hot and mild concoctions located on each table.

Having never advertised, the restaurant's 100 seats are filled by long-time customers and newcomers that have heard about the place from a friend. On weekends, about 50 percent of the business comes from Memphis, 35 miles away. Bozo's is open Monday through Saturday from 10:30 A.M. to 9:00 P.M., and offers the same menu items all day; (901) 294-3400.

Shelby County

With a population of about 700,000, Memphis rests along the Mississippi River and is one of the river's largest inland ports. Among many other things, the city is famous for its impact on the development of popular American music as well as the blues.

The history of music in the Memphis area revolves around the "King of Rock and Roll," Elvis Presley. Although he died in 1977, Elvis is more popular today; and his estate is worth much more now ($75 million) than it was when he died ($4.9 million), because of his home (Graceland Mansion), souvenir and tourist shops, and his museums. Estate revenues topped $15 million in 1989, more than the singer made in any one year of his career.

Each year in mid-August Memphis hosts the Elvis International Tribute Week, an action-packed week of events that include trivia contests, candelight vigils, special tours, tournaments, and parties. Humes Junior High School, where Elvis graduated from in 1953, is also open for tours and features a special exhibit room and a chance to walk across the stage where Elvis performed in a talent show.

Sun Studios, where Elvis recorded a song for his mother for $4, is open daily for tours on a year-round basis. Founded by disc jockey Sam Phillips, Sun was the first studio to record such musicians as Presley, Jerry Lee Lewis, Carl Perkins, and Johnny Cash. The studio is located at 706 Union Avenue, just a few blocks from Baptist Hospital, where Elvis was pronounced dead on August 16, 1977. Admission charged; (901) 521–0664.

Beale Street, in downtown Memphis, is considered the spiritual home of the other type of music the city is famous for, the blues. During its heyday in the twenties and thirties, there wasn't a tougher, more swinging street in America. The zoot suit originated here, and Machine Gun Kelly peddled bootleg on the streets. Always a mecca for musicians, the street's nightclubs were frequented by the country's best blues artists, including the man known as the Father of the Blues, the legendary William Christopher (W. C.) Handy.

Today, the street is once again a hot night spot, with numerous clubs, restaurants, and shops. But the sound of the blues has not been forgotten. Two clubs, Mr. Handy's Blues Hall (174 Beale) and the Rum Boogie Cafe (182 Beale) are still featuring traditional blues music.

Virtually unchanged through the years is Schwab's dry goods store, where a sign still hangs in the window proclaiming that "If you can't find it here, you're better off without it." The clerks still offer old-time service with a written receipt for each item purchased.

Downstairs, the Schwab family has created a museum. Having been on Beale Street since 1876, they have been able to collect quite a few memories of the "good ole days" to display. Upstairs, the store sells all sorts of items, from dream books to straw sailors to crystal balls to size 74 men's pants. Forty-Four kinds of suspenders are kept in stock.

The Memphis Police Museum is located at 159 Beale Street. It's located in an active police substation and is open every day, all day, all night. This precinct currently houses the walking, bicycle, and horse details for the Beale Street and downtown areas of the city.

Among other items, the museum has on tape the first car-to-car radio broadcast that took place in the city in 1940. Elvis also is saluted here. He was a reserve police captain, and the picture of him and his chief hangs on the walls. Next to it hangs the special orders taking him off the roll call following his death. Admission free; (901) 528–2370.

After wining and dining on Beale Street, head out to the airport where one of the most interesting industrial tours in the country begins weeknights at 11:30. Federal Express has its major hub here, and during the hour and a half that it will take you to walk through the facilities, jets will bring in more than 400,000 packages while 2,800 employees help sort them out and direct them in the right direction. Twenty-three miles of high-speed conveyer belts are used in the operation.

If it's history you came to Memphis for, take the short trip out to **Mud Island,** out in the Mississippi River across from downtown. The city has developed this area to display its rich river heritage. The River Walk is a five-block-long scale model of the entire Lower Mississippi's 1,000 miles from Cairo, Illinois, to the Gulf of Mexico. Every twist, turn, and split the river makes is shown on the model. Each step equals 1 mile along the mini-river, where each bridge and town is also depicted. Markers along the way point out interesting facts and figures. Water flows down the model into a one-acre Gulf of Mexico.

In 1989, sand was added to the 4-foot deep gulf and Boogie Beach was created. Now open for swimming, it's the largest swimming pool in the city.

The eighteen-gallery Mississippi River Museum is also located on the island and is a showcase for the people and the history of the river, with exhibits ranging from Indian arrowheads to a replica of the pilot house of a modern diesel towboat.

One of the galleries traces the wreck of the steamboat Sultana, which burned and sank nearby, killing 1,547 people. It is considered the worst maritime disaster in United States history. (901) 576–7241.

A visit to the **Peabody Hotel,** at 149 Union Street in downtown, is a must. Built in 1925, the grand hotel has been restored

The Peabody Ducks

and carries on a tradition started back in the mid-thirties. Each morning at eleven o'clock, five ducks are transported by elevator from their penthouse facilities to the lobby of the hotel.

As the doors slowly open, a red carpet is unrolled from the big fountain to the elevator as the King Cotton March is played over the sound system. With ranks of attending bellmen along both sides of the carpet, the ducks waddle to the fountain where they will spend the day. At 5:00 P.M., the action is reversed, and the ducks go back to their duck palace on the roof.

The palace is open to visitors, but that's not all you'll find up there. You'll also find a very impressive view of the river and downtown Memphis. (901) 529–4000.

Metalsmithing, everything from delicate gold jewelry to massive wrought-iron fencing, is the subject of one of the area's most unusual museums. Located in downtown Memphis on a bluff overlooking the Mississippi River, the National Ornamental Metal Museum was established in 1977 as a memorial to metalsmithing.

Changing exhibits are the basis of the museum, but its permanent collection contains a variety of items from jewelry to handmade nails to large outdoor sculptures to ancient iron locks. In the museum's smithy (anyplace where metal is worked) work is done daily by resident artists and members of museum classes. In October of each year, "Repair Days" is held. People from all over the South bring in their broken metal items to be fixed. On an average, thirty craftspeople are available during that time to repair "broken, bent or otherwise mutilated metalwork."

The museum grounds, at 374 West California, are a part of what was once known as the Marine Hospital, with the oldest of the three large brick buildings dating from 1870. That building was used in the extensive Memphis research that led to a cure for the yellow fever epidemics that once swept the area. The museum's main exhibit building was built as a Works Progress Administration project in 1932 and once served as a nurse's dormitory for the hospital complex. Admission is charged; (901) 774–6380.

Index

Acknowledgments

It's amazing how many people know so much, and it sure was nice that they all wanted to share that knowledge with a stranger.

As I drove the blue-line highways of the state of Tennessee searching for off-the-beaten-path sorts of things, I stopped and talked to many people, and to the best of my recollection each one I approached was able to help me in some fashion. It was from these people that I discovered many of the items in this book, and I thank them for their Southern hospitality.

I also wish to thank each and every employee of every chamber of commerce and tourism office I stopped at requesting information. They furnished a plethora of insightful local color.

Specifically, I want to thank Don Wick of the Tennessee Tourist Development office, Tom Adkinson of Opryland USA, and Richard Salisbury of the Tennessee Valley Authority for their leads, which opened many a door for me.

When people are willing to share their knowledge with others, it makes a job a lot easier. I couldn't have done it without a lot of help. Thanks to everyone!

About the Author

Tim O'Brien is a veteran news reporter and editor who now travels the world's highways and byways for a living as managing editor for *Amusement Business Newsweekly*. His specialty area of reportage is amusement parks and other types of tourist attractions.

When he's not traveling, he's at his home base near Nashville, Tennessee, where he lives with his wife, Rosi, and daughters, Carrie and Molly.

A graduate of Ohio State University with a Masters degree in Journalism/Film Production, Tim is also an accomplished photographer and a roller coaster fanatic, having ridden many of the world's greatest coasters.